Modern Rhododendrons

MODERN
RHODODENDRONS

E. H. M. COX and P. A. COX

With a foreword by
Dr J. M. COWAN V.M.H.

THOMAS NELSON AND SONS LTD
London Edinburgh Paris Melbourne Toronto and New York

THOMAS NELSON AND SONS LTD
Parkside Works Edinburgh 9
36 Park Street London W1
312 Flinders Street Melbourne C1

302–304 Barclays Bank Building
Commissioner and Kruis Streets
Johannesburg

THOMAS NELSON AND SONS (CANADA) LTD
91–93 Wellington Street West   Toronto 1

THOMAS NELSON AND SONS
19 East 47th Street New York 17

SOCIÉTÉ FRANÇAISE D'EDITIONS NELSON
25 rue Henri Barbusse Paris Vᵉ

———

First published 1956

To our long-suffering wife and mother
who listens without complaint
to hours of ' rhododendron ' talk,
so long as it is strictly forbidden
at mealtimes

Preface

We have great pleasure in presenting this manuscript to the Garden Committee of the National Trust of Scotland.

We have to thank friends for answers readily given to many questions. Among these are Mrs Roza Stevenson and Mr H. H. Davidian. Particularly are we grateful to Dr J. M. Cowan v.m.h., for reading the proofs and providing a Foreword. Finally we are more than indebted to Miss Margaret Stones for her charming drawings in black-and-white and colour which form the illustrations to this volume.

E. H. M. COX
P. A. COX

Glendoick, Perth
November 1955

Contents

List of Coloured Plates

List of Text Illustrations

Foreword

To the authors' proposal that I should equip this book with a foreword I was, for several good reasons, more than ready to agree.

Firstly, because a book of this kind is badly needed. *Modern Rhododendrons* will, I believe, be greatly in demand; for, with all the newer introductions, the many species and the still more numerous recent hybrids that may be grown today are bewildering in their multitude and diversity.

' Which of them shall I take? Both? one? or neither? ' This, in King Lear, was Edmund's problem, for he had dallied with both daughters, Regan and Goneril; but the dilemma in which the rhododendron lover finds himself is far more complex!

Here, then, in *Modern Rhododendrons* valuable guidance is provided for those who wish to make a selection—larger or smaller—or to become better acquainted with the more worthy of their choice.

There is nothing quite like *Modern Rhododendrons*, of the same compass and in the same convenient form, for the *Species of Rhododendron*, except for the specialist, is too abstruse, and Millais' two large volumes, *Rhododendrons*, even if they can be bought, are suited neither to the pocket nor the purse. Moreover, neither of these works is now fully up to date, and the *Rhododendron Handbook*, far less discriminating, lacks the personal touch.

Modern Rhododendrons is a short treatise, readable, well-timed and to the point, dealing with species and hybrids alike ; though with the emphasis (and rightly, I think) upon the species.

What is the criterion of a modern rhododendron ? It is said that a man's age is what he feels his age to be, so, I suppose, we are entitled to assume that modern rhododendrons are as modern as you care to make them. Anyhow, I am glad to see that the title does not confine the authors to the latest introductions and the newest hybrids. It may be remarked that even the most venerable of the species, *R. ferrugineum*, the Alpine Rose, comes under review, and honourable veterans, known for over a century, are not cast out.

No ! *Modern Rhododendrons* is a comprehensive survey. All rhododendrons (species and hybrids) deemed worth while having in a modern garden are included, and they have been selected by experienced growers and are described by connoisseurs.

I commend, too, the lists at the end of the book—twelve lists, each of twelve rhododendrons. These are suggestions as to what to select for planting in various situations, in the larger and the smaller garden, in the woodland or in the rock garden or for their striking foliage and so on. Of course, no-one familiar with rhododendrons will agree with these lists—anyhow not entirely—but they are a sound guide for the novice. They are certain, as the authors predict, to raise discussion, but, as they say, it has been fun making them, and it will be fun picking them to pieces and remaking them. For all that, I believe my own adjudication would not be so very different in the end.

Secondly, I was ready to co-operate because it is a pleasure to be associated with friends. In the authorship of this book we have an unusual and happy combination,

for father and son are a rare co-partnership in an enterprise
of this kind.

The elder, as many people know, has a wide knowledge
of rhododendrons and a long experience, and is familiar
with them not only in the gardens of this country and in
the United States of America, but also as they grow in their
native land, for he accompanied Farrer in Burma. Moreover, as an author he is well known by his book, *Farrer's
Last Journey*, and by numerous other works. The younger
is no less enthusiastic, and he too has had the opportunity
of visiting many of the noteworthy gardens where rhododendrons predominate. Both have the good fortune to share
in common a delightful garden in the east of Scotland, where
the successful cultivation of rhododendrons is, however, much
more difficult and limited than in the west. From this it
follows that anything they may recommend as having been
grown by themselves is likely to be robust.

Finally, I was the more pleased to become associated
with this book, because the authors have most generously
agreed to give the manuscript to the Gardens Committee
of the National Trust for Scotland, in which Mr Cox senior
succeeded me as Vice-Convener. This Committee is now
responsible for the wellbeing and maintenance of such far-
famed gardens as Inverewe and Crathes on behalf of the
Trust, and contributions to its funds are greatly welcomed.
It has also as its aim the building up of a fund which could
provide an endowment for any celebrated garden in Scotland which might become dependent upon the Trust for its
future preservation.

J. M. COWAN

Inverewe, Poolewe
Wester Ross
November 1955

xiii

Introduction

WE have written this book on modern rhododendrons as a possible help to others who have or may become rhododendron enthusiasts. The older one of us has retained his enthusiasm for more than thirty years. His initial desire to grow everything that bears the name of rhododendron has faded to a rather belated recognition that all is not gold that glitters, with the result that he hopes that his judgment is a little sounder and a little less exuberant. The younger of us has all the enthusiasms of youth tempered by knowledge gained, among other places, at the Royal Botanic Garden, Edinburgh, where every spare moment over two years was spent in that famous Mecca of rhododendron enthusiasts.

One thing both of us have learnt, that far from becoming less complicated as time goes on, the nomenclature of cultivated species of rhododendron is becoming more involved. As new introductions become better known, and the very large amount of dried herbarium material is critically examined, it is becoming obvious that many of the plants originally given specific names form such close alliances that in their natural state they are really what can be called natural hybrids. In other words their characters are not sufficiently fixed for them to be given specific rank. This examination is still being carried on, and it may be years before a final opinion is reached. Examples of this confusion are to be found in such series as the *Cinnabarinum* and the *Lapponicum*, and the *Sanguineum* subseries of the *Neriiflorum* series.

This makes the task of selection even more difficult for the beginner. He may admire rhododendron A in a friend's garden, but on ordering A he may find, after waiting for it to flower for several years, that his A is not even in the same range of colour. Although possibly more prevalent, this, of course, is nothing new. The old Himalayan *R. campanulatum*, for instance, is a very variable plant. Well over a century ago it had a wave of popularity, particularly in Scotland, and many hundreds of seedlings were planted. While it can be one of the most charming of the larger growing species with flowers sometimes of a deep lavender-blue that is shown off so well by the tawny indumentum on the undersurface of the leaves, it can also be a hideous magenta with poorly shaped trusses. Today there are a dozen mediocre forms to be seen in old gardens to every one of the attractive shades. But at least that was one plant with one name. Today it is unfortunate that in many cases several plants are in cultivation which have been given specific rank with only minute botanical differences, such as the presence or absence of glands on their ovaries.

We have, therefore, tried to be fair and give warning either by mentioning a close resemblance between two or more plants or by listing what is probably the best in a close alliance and ignoring the rest.

Our criteria of hardiness do not always coincide with those who grow rhododendrons farther south or west, but we always imagine, possibly rightly, possibly wrongly, that anything that will survive our east coast climate for several years will grow equally well in any other part of the British Isles where it is possible to grow rhododendrons.

There are those who prefer a ready-made garden where everything that is growing is as foolproof as possible, where nothing is planted that may be damaged by frost, where gardening is made easy. Those are not the gardeners who, as Reginald Farrer wrote: feel ' the throb and thrill of Spring. Oh, don't I know it ! For that is what turns my heart to the hills in June, and what, in the first warm days of March, sets me itching to get my fingers into the vibrations of the awakening earth.'

Growing rhododendrons in other parts of the country than the very lush and very mild extreme west and south-west is, to a certain extent, a battle of wits ; for gardening, as we see it, must be partly imaginative. While we like looking at a meticulous array in a completed and a trouble-free garden, we would not care to own one. There is so much to be learned and such a short span in which to learn. For the real enthusiast no garden is ever complete ; and Heaven forbid that it ever should be.

If you look up a Dictionary of Botanic Terms, under the word *lepidote* you will find ' beset with small scurfy scales '. It is this definition that divides the great Genus Rhododendron into two wide sections : the first, the lepidote series, with scales ; the second, the elepidote series, without scales. This great division is not arbitrary, as with one or two very rare exceptions species from one group will not hybridise with any species from the other group. One exception, a hybrid called Grierdal, made rhododendron history, as it is the first recorded definite hybrid between a lepidote species, *R. dalhousiae*, and an elepidote species, *R. griersonianum*. The result is half-way between the two species, even if it is not particularly attractive.

The further division of the genus into series has not been an easy task. Although these divisions have been made as natural as possible, in some cases the results cannot but be arbitrary. The series, as at present constituted, are as follows :

Lepidote Series

Anthopogon	Lepidotum
Boothii	Maddenii
Camelliaeflorum	Micranthum
Campylogynum	Moupinense
Carolinianum	Saluenense
Cinnabarinum	Scabrifolium
Dauricum	Trichocladum
Edgeworthii	Triflorum
Ferrugineum	Uniflorum
Glaucophyllum	Vaccinioides
Heliolepis	Virgatum
Lapponicum	

Elipidote Series

Albiflorum	Grande
Arboreum	Irroratum
Auriculatum	Lacteum
Azalea	Neriiflorum
Barbatum	Ovatum
Campanulatum	Ponticum
Camtschaticum	Semibarbatum
Falconeri	Stamineum
Fortunei	Taliense
Fulvum	Thomsonii

Cultivation

ON looking back over the years any gardener who has made a point of visiting collections of rhododendrons must call to mind some particular plant or group of plants that held his attention. Such plants will remain clear in his memory as being remarkably well grown. As examples we can recall a magnificent specimen of *R. orbiculare* that almost filled a tiny sand-pit at Caerhays Castle in Cornwall, a 25-foot tree of an old hybrid very close to true *R. arboreum* in a wood at Balbirnie in Fife, a huge plant of *R. forrestii* sprawling on a bank at Tower Court near Ascot, and the well-known hedge of *R. x praecox* in all its early glory at the Royal Botanic Garden in Edinburgh ; all of them plants that were not only happily placed but were so obviously in a state of health beyond the ordinary.

No one garden can be specially favoured in every rhododendron that it grows, nor can definite rules be laid down for their more or less successful cultivation under every condition. If all rules of cultivation were cut and dried, half the fun and most of the excitement in growing rhododendrons would disappear. When the first great flow of new species began to reach our gardens from China and south-east Tibet, gardeners imagined that hard and fast rules could be evolved which would cover all the plants then known. Did not collectors' field notes describe plants that came from rain forests under the constant influence of the monsoon, and others that came from cold and draughty uplands or from drier regions of the Mekong-Yangtze divide, and so on ? At home we began to translate those descriptions into terms consistent with our own knowledge and our own particular conditions : and in many cases we were wrong.

Shade and Shelter

One of the most difficult aspects of cultivation about which to generalise is shade. In the early days we were always being warned about the importance of shade for all rhododendrons except the cast-iron hybrids and the dwarf species from the Chinese moors that take the place there of our native heather. And yet we are perfectly certain that we ourselves have lost more plants from growing them in too much shade than in too little. During five years of war no-one went near our rhododendron glen. When we came back in 1945, it was a tangle of birch and bramble that had smothered dozens of plants, mostly by closing in above the rhododendrons and keeping off almost all sunlight. That was an extreme case. But we defy anyone to be dogmatic and lay down quarter- or half- or three-quarters-shade. How can anyone compare shade in Benmore in Argyll with more than a hundred inches of rain in the year, as wet in summer as in winter, with that in Ascot with twenty or so inches and a summer heat that may be in the high seventies for almost weeks on end ; or that in the coastal Cornish gardens with a high humidity whatever the temperature, with that in Portland, Oregon, which has a rainfall of forty inches which almost all falls between October and March, and experiences drought conditions during late summer and early autumn ?

It cannot be done, this generalising about shade. Gardeners must use their own judgment, and beginners should visit other rhododendron gardens during high summer and compare conditions with what they can provide. All

6

that can be said is that some shade is necessary for most species and the more modern hybrids, and that shade from the early morning sun is much more important than that from the evening sun, particularly in areas where ground frosts are prevalent.

To begin with we followed the advice that used to be given. In our glen the shade from surrounding trees is such that four hours of sunshine a day is the maximum that any plant could expect. But at the start we were imbued with this absolute necessity for shade. Not satisfied with what we had, we planted a number of birch and large shrubs like the taller-growing cotoneasters and viburnums. During the past ten years some of our time has been spent in removing much of this top hamper and giving our rhododendrons more sunshine. They are healthier as a result, and in particular have a greater chance to ripen their wood and produce more flower buds. But what is suitable here in east Perthshire would certainly not prove satisfactory either in Benmore or in Ascot.

There is another point, the shape in which you want your Rhododendrons to grow. Let us give an example. Near Hpimaw in Upper Burma grew one of the *Irroratum* series, *R. tanastylum*, with glowing deep-red flowers. It was fairly plentiful from about 8,000 to 9,000 feet, but in the rain forest it had always a long straggling stem of twenty or more feet with a bunch of leaves and a few flowers searching for a break in the thick canopy overhead. We saw, however, one plant in a natural clearing where a forest giant had crashed a few years before, and regeneration for some reason was only low scrub. Here *R. tanastylum* was a shapely bush, about six feet high, clothed almost to the ground and with forty or fifty trusses in full flower. What had been very

7

uninspiring had become exciting. That may be an extreme
case, but it has given us a permanent dislike of long drawn
up ' Alices '. We saw one or two gardens in the United
States where they seemed to like plants that were long and
lanky, and there are many gardeners in this country who are
not so particular as they might be about the correct pro-
portions of their plants. We would recommend them to visit
Inverewe in Ross-shire. This sea-shore garden has suffered
during the past year or two from excessive wind, which has
blown down some of the very necessary shelter. But one of the
joys of this garden is the sense of well-being and proportion
of most of the individual plants. The late Mrs Sawyer
planted her rhododendrons far wider apart than is normal
practice, and would move them without hesitation on the
slightest appearance of overcrowding. The result of this
wise policy is that there are few plants which are not shapely
and well clothed almost to the ground. Many of our west-
coast gardens possess acres in which to expand : in smaller
gardens it is not so easy to achieve this individual comeliness
without possibly having to sacrifice something else ; and the
choice may be difficult.

The provision of actual shelter is often a matter of
personal ingenuity if it is required in a hurry. Bamboo
screening, wattle hurdles and so on, all have their uses, while
more permanent shelter is growing. Shade is a long-term
policy and requires more thought. An old oak wood is the
ideal, followed by Scots pine or even sweet chestnut. We
are suspicious of birch, partly because of the nuisance of
self-sown seedlings and partly because they are undoubtedly
greedy plants. Beech is, of course, impossible. Elm and
sycamore, which we have to suffer, are greedy shallow
rooters, and insects on the foliage of an old sycamore seem

to exude a sticky gum that disfigures every rhododendron leaf under it.

Those of us with collections of more or less mature rhododendrons suffer from an additional disadvantage. We had to start, as it were, from scratch owing to ignorance of the garden value of these new discoveries. George Forrest collected *R. beesianum*, a rather dull member of the *Lacteum* series, and sent home dried material, under no less than forty-one numbers ; and of many of these numbers seed was also sent home. The enthusiast with many acres of woodland to fill might have been able to deal with a plant or two from each collector's number, but what was the poor individual to do who at the most had two or three acres which could be planted with rhododendrons ? It was a hit or miss affair up to well on in the 1930's ; bigger growers could juggle with their plants like pieces of a jigsaw puzzle, but those of us with limited areas were often unable to fit our plants into the landscape as we should have liked. In a large area a group of one of the less exciting *Taliense* series would look quite attractive in a suitable setting, whereas one plant that could easily be compared with more attractive neighbours would look excessively dowdy. Thus all we could do was to be ruthless and throw away those that obviously looked very poor or very dull.

That paragraph is preparatory to saying that no-one today who wishes to start even the smallest collection of rhododendrons has the same excuse. Any that he will start with will be starred in the *Rhododendron Handbook* to show their value in the rhododendron hierarchy. He can see mature plants growing and flowering in gardens. He can go to nurseries and pick his plants. The modern gardener has no excuse if he does not fit his rhododendrons into the landscape and does not visualise, at least in part, what they will look like in a few years' time.

In a genus of such diversity it is impossible to lay down on paper even suggestions about planting to fit the landscape. In the old days, with the constant arrival of fresh consignments of seed, excess plants were often used for shelter belts or background planting. We ourselves, more by luck than good guidance, once used an excess of *R. desquamatum* for such a purpose. They are now fifteen or more feet high and are very good value.

With increased costs and shortage of labour such specific plantings may today be considered extravagant, but much more could be made of existing stands of *R. ponticum* or old hybrids of *R. catawbiense* that exist in the areas round so many old gardens. They make the very best shelter, if bays are cut out of them. The soil is often full of humus. In themselves they make a good background, particularly for large-leaved species where the comparison between the size of the leaves is most striking. The only labour is to keep the thickets of *R. ponticum* cut back, and this is better done annually.

In all cases shelter should be given from the prevailing wind or winds. In Scotland this should be given against winds from the east and north-west, and shade from the early morning sun. But beware of shelter that may be a frost pocket. If the garden is on a slope, we are all of us inclined to move downhill for shelter and so may enter a pocket. In woodland these are often very deceptive, so much so that now we use a set of synchronised thermometers before we bring in any new area for planting. They are very useful instruments, simple glass tubes which are set in forked twigs horizontal to and a few inches above the ground. They show the minimum and not the maximum temperature.

This shelter from an east wind is of great importance anywhere near the east coast. There is a garden near with a fine group of *R. x praecox*, that lovely early hybrid. It is planted on a slope, most of it facing south and protected from the east, but with a few plants round a corner facing east and north-east. As a March-flowering rhododendron *R. praecox* is liable to be cut in flower, although moderately bud-hardy. In this garden it escapes severe frosting during flowering possibly three years out of five when there is a fine show on the plants facing south, but there is never more than an odd flower or two even in a most favourable season on the plants facing east. We have a cold, biting, drying wind that blasts flowers and flower-buds far more quickly than several degrees of ground frost. If shelter from the east wind cannot be provided, it is better to grow something other than rhododendrons. It is a wise gardener that knows his damaging wind !

Soil

It is always said that rhododendrons along with almost all other *Ericaceae* will not grow in an alkaline soil. Soil chemists use a *p*H scale to denote degrees of alkalinity and acidity, with *p*H7 as neutral, *p*H6 as slightly acid, *p*H8 as slightly alkaline. The scale is logarithmic. Thus *p*H5 is ten times more acid than *p*H6, and *p*H9 ten times more alkaline than *p*H8. Dr Tod at the East of Scotland College of Agriculture has been experimenting with the alkalinity that rhododendrons will stand, and has found that this depends not on the *p*H value so much as on the calcium content. In other words rhododendrons will grow in a soil that is *p*H8 provided that the alkalinity is caused by magnesium and not by calcium. He has grown and flowered rhododendrons successfully for six years in pots in a magnesium-induced soil of *p*H8.

There is considerable difference of opinion about the degree of acidity necessary. Personally we think that it does not matter, with a few exceptions, so long as there is plenty of humus present in the soil. In these days of shortage of natural fertilisers and natural humus all kinds of substitutes have been tried; mill dust from textile mills and wool shoddy are examples of materials that take a long time to break down in the soil, and in the process use up a large amount of the available nitrogen. There have been cases of gardeners so desperate for humus that they have incorporated fresh straw and chopped bracken in the soil without allowing time for it to weather as a mulch. Quite apart from the time that must elapse before it disintegrates into useful humus, the act of breaking down such fibres in the soil will again use up much of the available nitrogen, and the soil will be all that poorer for the time being.

A light soil is undoubtedly better for rhododendrons than a heavy one. As they are known to be surface rooters, many gardeners pay little attention to the subsoil when planting; but that is a mistake, as good drainage is of the utmost importance, and that depends largely on the state of the subsoil. This is particularly important where a hard pan exists a foot or two down. In all cases it is safer after digging a hole to work the subsoil over thoroughly with a pick or mattock.

Another item in preparing the soil that we think important is the thorough incorporation of whatever is thought a necessary addition to the existing soil. We know that some gardeners with a not very kindly soil will dig out a hole a little larger than the root system and fill it with a suitable soil mixture. When the fibrous roots reach the outside perimeter of the hole, they almost always refuse to penetrate anything stickier or harder or colder if the change from one soil condition to another is sudden. If it is impossible to lighten a heavy soil over a large area, the two different textures must be well mixed with a fork where they meet.

We have seen it suggested more than once that in heavy soils rhododendrons, particularly hybrids, should be planted in raised mounds of a suitable mixture. This we consider to be a great mistake, unless in areas of a heavy rainfall. As they are shallow rooters, it is better to plant them in a saucer where a suitable mulch can be added, the only point, of course, being that drainage is as good as possible.

Feeding

It is also wrong to imagine that rhododendrons can live and thrive in drier districts in the very poorest of soils without feeding. This is of particular importance in old gardens where a shrub has been removed that has been growing in one place for years without any additional nourishment, and a rhododendron is planted in its place. We know that in a number of the larger collections no rhododendron is planted without having at least one forkful of well-rotted farmyard manure incorporated in the soil in which it is planted. If this is unobtainable, a double handful of some slow-acting fertiliser, such as hoof and horn plus peat and leaf mould, should be added to the soil round a large plant. We have a hungry soil with many tree roots, and we find that all our rhododendrons are the better for a little stimulant each year. When we have it, we like to give them an annual handful or two of a mixture that we use on our raspberry field, five parts of fish guano, three parts of superphosphate and two parts of sulphate of potash. But any standard garden fertiliser will do so long as it contains sulphate of potash and not muriate of potash. Garden compost is also good, so long as it has not been activated with any kind of lime. We apply any of these fertilisers just before the growing season.

We try and give a mulch of some kind to keep up the humus content in our hungry soil, but it is difficult in a glen such as we possess with steep banks to keep this as high as we should like. There is one point about a mulch that some gardeners are inclined to forget. Unless the mulch itself has feeding value, such as good leaf mould, its value to the rhododendron is almost completely mechanical. Humus is not necessarily a term for plant-food. It will help in conserving moisture, and will ultimately break down and become a rooting medium ; but if the soil is deficient in plant-food, humus may not add sufficient for the well-being of the rhododendron population.

This problem of feeding is probably more acute on the east coast of Scotland than on the west or in the southern half of England. It is unfortunate that our dry period, with very low humidity, usually corresponds with what should be the time of maximum growth. In other areas with a much heavier rainfall and far greater humidity, vegetation breaks down more quickly and returns to the soil as humus. This increased humus and greater humidity and warmth gives the necessary impetus to a quick and sturdy growth, an impetus that we often lack.

We deliberately encourage a ground cover of weeds during our spring. Where they begin to become a nuisance they are scythed twice in the season in mid-May and again at the end of July. As far as possible nettles are not allowed. These are kept down with sodium chlorate, which oddly enough we find has little or no effect on rhododendrons. We spray sodium chlorate regularly within three feet of the outside perimeter of a well-grown plant and have never found it to be any the worse. We have a number of maples among the rhododendrons, and these we find extremely susceptible. We cannot use sodium chlorate within twelve feet of any maple.

Variation in the nutritional value of soils can take place within a very few feet. We have a perfect example near our glen. Some rhododendrons are planted in what was once an old orchard. The fruit trees were grubbed up many years ago, but the loam is deep and holds the moisture fairly well, while analysis show that the soil is average. Just across the path not ten feet away the soil is invaded by roots of two or three old spruce and elms which have sucked out any goodness there might have been in it years ago. This area not only has to be fed constantly, but also watered almost for days on end, if the rhododendrons planted there are to make any show of growth at all. If it were not that the landscape needs some rhododendrons in this area to fill rather an ugly foreground, we would leave it alone. We know that the work entailed in looking after a dozen more or less mature specimens is more than looking after a hundred elsewhere.

Pruning and Thinning

While most rhododendrons are sociable plants, they suffer as much, if not more, from overcrowding as any other shrubs. On the other hand they have the advantage over most other woody plants that almost all of them can be moved at any age during the dormant season. Thus there is little excuse for thin mis-shapen plants if care has been taken to preserve their shape when younger. It is, of course, obvious that clumps of the old cast-iron hybrids are as natural and as good looking as an interwoven carpet of dwarfs. No-one can deny that any of the members of the large-leaved series the arboreums, the grandes and the falconeris are much better seen in a solitary state whether they are grown as a bush or dendriform. So is the type of rhododendron with stout branches that form a definite pattern like *R. thomsonii*. And it is just the members of these series that do not take at all kindly to being cut about with a knife ; in fact few, if any will break into new wood at all below where a major branch has been removed.

On the other hand dwarfs and most lepidotes like members of the large *Triflorum* series will break freely ; indeed dwarfs that are tending to grow out of character owing to too much shade or too wet a season are all the better for being clipped just after flowering and before growth has commenced.

A word of warning should be given about grafted plants. If these are cut back too hard, there is a danger of the graft dying and suckers in quantity appearing from the root system. In all groups of commercial hybrids of standard varieties a close watch should be kept to see that *ponticum* suckers do not take control. There are many old gardens with clumps of enormous size of *R. ponticum* or *R. catawbiense* where these were originally planted as groups of mixed hybrids, and in every case the graft has died out. If root grafting were to come into more general practice the danger would not be so great, but it would still be present.

We are often asked if dead-heading is necessary for their

health. The answer is probably no. If a plant looks un-
healthy and carries a disproportionate amount of flowers,
the damage has already been done. There is a theory that
most of the plant's energy is spent in producing pollen and
not seed. A plant that is sick will often try to perpetuate
itself by producing an abnormal amount of flower-buds.
We are always suspicious when this occurs and try and
remove as many as possible before the flowers open.

But that is not to say that dead-heading is not sometimes
necessary. Most rhododendron seed-heads are very persistent
and are by no means beautiful. Anything dead left on a
plant may become a host for an insect or fungus spores. If
seed heads are left on, more growth-buds may grow from their
base than usual with an excess of branchlets the following
year, possibly many of them growing in a direction which is
not consistent with the general shape of the plant. Naturally
in a large collection, particularly where there are large-sized
plants, it is impossible to dead head every plant. We start,
with those that have the largest seed heads and work down
the scale as far as we are able.

Watering

This depends on climate and water supply. It is, of course,
an advantage when the growing season coincides with dry
weather and low humidity as so often happens in our part of
Scotland. We usually get a wet July and a dry May and
June. If plants are thrown out of the rhythm of their normal
growth by drought conditions and then are soaked for weeks
on end, they may start into a second growth that rarely
comes to anything. And almost always such conditions
means an absence of flower during the following year.

We are lucky in having water laid on with more than

twenty-five pounds pressure. Thus we can use a water fan. If this is left on one area overnight and the ground thoroughly soaked, we find that one watering will usually carry the plants through a normal dry spell, and is sufficient to enable them to complete their growth, although it may not be quite so vigorous as under natural conditions. Watering like that is much better than watering a plant for a few minutes at shorter intervals. We would like to comment, however, on a practice that we saw carried out in several gardens in the north-western United States, that of watering right on to the end of October. With their hotter and much drier summers watering is essential if rhododendrons are to grow well, but rhododendrons, like most other woody plants, are all the better for a dry period during which they can ripen the wood made during the past growing season. In several of these gardens in Seattle and Portland sprinklers were going full at the end of October with young wood as green and as sappy as if they were in mid-growth. The consequence was that many large and mature plants were carrying far too few flowers for their size and age. During the winter months these gardens get anything up to thirty inches of rain ; and this autumn watering is quite unnecessary.

MARGARET STONES

Rhododendron neriiflorum

Propagation

THE focus of rhododendron propagation has altered in the past fifteen years. While collectors were at work in the Far East and in the Himalayas, there was a steady flow home of rhododendron seed. As much of it was of unknown quality, the amount of seed sown by rhododendron enthusiasts was enormous, in many cases out of all proportion to the ultimate value of the flowering plant. But growers were afraid to hold their hand in case something superlatively good was missed. Thus in the first three decades of the century the focus was almost entirely on seeds and seedlings, to begin with very largely of species, while a little later, after Forrest's death and the flow of new material from the Far East began to dry up, the emphasis turned more to the production of hybrids.

It was only after this mass of new material, whether species or hybrid, began to be digested in our gardens that growers began to concentrate on the increase of special forms of species and of particularly fine hybrids. This increase of existing plants is, of course, only possible by vegetative means, by cuttings and layers, and to a lesser extent by grafts. Almost all the so-called hardy hybrids produced commercially are grafted plants.

One of the difficulties that lies before the modern propagator whether amateur or professional, is the fact that there are very few, if any, rhododendron species where every seed that was sent home has produced a flowering plant that is indistinguishable from its neighbours. Rhododendron exhibits have proved this variation time and again, a variation that cannot be accounted for entirely by the climate and cultivation in one garden being superior to those of another. There are good forms and poor forms of almost every species. In addition, during the heyday of plant collecting in the Far East, systematic botanists who examined the dried material sent home over a number of years were unable to check their findings until a whole range of garden-grown specimens of flowering size were available. There is no possible doubt that far too many new species were named and their descriptions published. What were then counted as new species are now being sunk into varietal forms of other species or merely classed as synonyms.

But they do differ, even in slight degrees, and this is clearly seen in the progeny produced by controlled hybridisation. A very good example is *R. x loderi*. This was first produced by Sir Edmund Loder in 1907 by crossing *R. griffithianum* and *R. fortunei*. An earlier form of the same cross was made at Kew in 1888 and called *R. x kewense*, and it has been repeated several times after 1907. But in no case is the progeny equal to the hybrids made by Sir Edmund Loder, owing to the special qualities of the plants used as parents. This variation is also shown by the fact that *R. x kewense* is a better plant in our harder and drier climate in the east coast of Scotland than *R. x loderi*, which thrives under moister conditions than we can often give it.

We stress this point to show how necessary vegetative propagation is if particular plants have to be increased. We have met one or two enthusiasts since World War II who still imagine that a seed-pod picked from species A growing and flowering in the middle of other rhododendrons will produce hundreds of other little A's all alike as two peas. The chances are extremely unlikely.

There is nothing really new in modern propagation of rhododendrons. There are a few refinements in growing from seed, and more is known about the best time to take cuttings of various series, but the underlying basis for all propagating methods remain the same. What is different is the switch from one method to another. As the technique of rooting cuttings improves, fewer plants are grown from layers, a slow, laborious and often unsightly method of increase. The commercial grafting of standard hybrids continues in the trade, as it is still the cheapest and quickest method of bulk increase. The controlled selfing of species that are difficult to propagate by vegetative means is increasing. This is particularly the case with species and series that will not respond to propagation by cuttings and are too large and stiff to layer. The *Falconeri* series and the *Thomsonii* subseries of the *Thomsonii* series are examples. Two *R. thomsonii* are crossed with each other under conditions where the flowers cannot be contaminated by outside pollen. The resultant seed is pure *R. thomsonii*. In many cases the children of these crosses have proved hardier and more vigorous with better flowers than the parents. The only point, of course, is that a number of years must elapse before these children come to flowering size. It is, however, a much better method than the sowing of seed from seed-pods picked haphazardly and then labelled with the seed-parent's name, which may be crossed, not with the same species, but with something else growing near by.

Propagation by means of seed

The germination of rhododendron seed under one year old presents no difficulties. What is not so easy is to bring the newly germinated seedlings through the first week or two of their lives. When the late Harry White was in charge of the Sunningdale Nurseries, he raised all his rhododendron seedlings in frames sunk in the pine-needled floor of his woodland nursery. There may have been lights on them in bad weather, but we cannot recall ever having seen them in use. This method of open-air germination certainly made for sturdy and healthy seedlings. The dappled shade thrown by the large Scots pines was sufficient without being too dark, and damping off was almost unknown. This is possible in the warmer counties of southern England where the soil is sufficiently acid to restrict the growth of annual weeds, but it is too slow farther north or where the rainfall is excessive.

Where we have to raise our rhododendron seedlings in a greenhouse, the main improvement in technique is in the interior propagating frame with electrical soil heating. This can be used for raising seedlings or soft-wood or medium hard-wood cuttings, but not both at the same time in the same frame. Unlike many improvements it is cheap to instal. The kind that we use is a 40-foot plastic-covered heating element. The frame is 12 inches at the back and 9 inches in front and is laid direct on the slate bench in the green-house. On the top of the slate is 1 inch of broken crocks, covered with gravel or very coarse sand. Above this is a 5-inch layer of half-fine peat and half-sharp sand. The heating element is laid 4 inches down, with 1 inch of the rooting mixture below. It is advisable to have the frame thermostatically controlled, as with tight-fitting lights on top of the frame the heat generated may become excessive, particularly if the sun suddenly appears with inadequate winter shading. The current used in the 40-foot is about 300 watts. The heating element can be used in various sizes of frame. For our purpose when extreme heat is not desired we use it in a frame 12 ft. by 3 ft. Thus it covers 36 square feet. If more heat is required the heating element is laid out to cover a frame 6 ft. by 3 ft., thus covering 18 square feet.

In this propagating frame we place our seed pans. Any number of suggestions have been made of different sowing mediums for the seeds of rhododendrons, chopped sphagnum, chopped Osmunda fibre, John Innes compost, and so on. We have tried a number, but have come to the conclusion that under any conditions the most suitable is pure, finely sieved peat moss, with nothing added. It is packed down fairly tightly in the pan and well soaked with rain-water. The rhododendron seed is then thinly sown on the top and is left uncovered. (We stress *thinly*.) The pans are syringed and the frames closed. All seed pans are syringed daily. The frames are kept closed until germination is well advanced, usually in ten to fifteen days, when the pans are removed to another frame where more and more air is given them each day, and also light so long as they are shaded from the direct rays of the sun. Whenever the main germination is in progress we sieve a little very fine peat or sand over the surface of the pans.

When they have germinated about a month we syringe once a fortnight with an extremely dilute liquid manure instead of plain water.

We like peat as we are certain there is less chance of damping off, being almost sterile there are few weeds, and particularly because pricking-off can be done with little root damage. There is one point, however ; when any transplanting has to be done with plants like rhododendrons with a fine fibrous root system, the texture of the soil into which they are transplanted should be as similar as possible to that in which they were previously grown. Thus we cannot use in pricking-off anything like the John Innes potting compost as it is usually made up. We use one part of peat, one of coarse sand, one of loam and one of finely sifted leaf mould. We prick seedlings into this as soon as they can be conveniently handled. Seedlings should not be pricked off into too great a depth of soil. The average depth of soil in our boxes is 2½ inches. We see no advantage in sowing rhododendron seed in pans filled to the brim with the sowing mixture, a practice advocated by some authorities.

Whatever the seedling may be, we like to harden them off behind a north wall or in fairly deep shade for at least part of the summer once their first main growth is completed.

May we give one word of warning to all who live near the sea, or close to an estuary or other salt water. Be careful to see that your sand is not dredged from salt or brackish water. Salt may take a long time to leach out of the sand even if left in the open ; and salty sand in the compost is one of the best and quickest methods of killing young rhododendrons.

One other point ; see that your rhododendron seed is as clean as possible before sowing. Bits of old seed husk sown with the seed is one of the quickest methods of bringing mould into a seed-pan.

There is a great deal to be said for bringing on rhododendron seedlings as quickly as possible. If tiny seedlings are allowed to grow too slowly, there comes a time when they appear to stick for weeks, particularly if they have been allowed to get and remain dry for a day or two. On the whole they are gregarious plants in the young stage and, within moderation like to be in a crowd. If they are brought on quickly, they will almost certainly make a second growth during the same season and much time will be saved. But these forced seedlings should always be brought into a cold frame or house for their first winter after hardening off outside.

If it is at all possible use rain-water. Our tap-water comes from a dam that is full of algae ; when our rain-water runs short and we have to use tap-water, the tops of the seed pans are soon covered with a matted green scum. Our water supply in the greenhouses may be particularly bad in that respect, but all tap-water is suspect even if it is kept in a greenhouse tank to warm up to greenhouse temperature ; and rhododendron seedlings resent copper sulphate at a strength sufficient to keep down the algae.

A useful aid in a propagating house is a thin sheeting of polythene tacked to the astragals, leaving an air space between it and the glass. The plastic sheeting acts in more or less the same way as a vacuum flask. (A special plastic sheeting is now manufactured for the purpose.) This lets through about 95 per cent. of the light. Tests show that a greenhouse thus sheeted is at least 6 degrees warmer in winter and the same amount cooler in summer. This provides a more equable temperature at a very low cost, as well as showing a distinct saving in heating in winter in a house that only aims at keeping the frost out.

Grafting

Grafting is more of a commercial method of rhododendron propagation than one used by amateurs. It certainly requires more manual skill and practice than any other. As a rule grafted plants are disliked by gardeners owing to their habit of suckering. As a stock plant *R. ponticum* has been used for more than a century, and its use is likely to continue as there is no rhododendron which is more amenable to any kind of lime-free soil, and few which are better able to withstand extremes of exposure. But many of the huge clumps of *R. ponticum* that exist throughout the country started life as one or other of the old hybrids of cast-iron constitution. In course of time the stock began to sucker and the grafted scion was smothered out.

We know an area of about ten acres of *R. ponticum* where a bulldozer would be necessary to clear a path : yet we remember our father and grandfather respectively, telling us that in the early eighties this used to be a thin and pleasant woodland, with glades lined by what was then an excellent collection of new hybrid rhododendrons. Today not one remains, but mounds of *R. ponticum* 12 feet high and 30 feet through, joining and interlacing with each other to such an extent that it is quite impossible to force a way through. And that is no solitary case.

Although commercial grafting is still carried on to a large extent by nurserymen in Holland and Belgium, modern hybrids, where possible, are increased in the British Isles by layers or cuttings. Some experts believe that plants grafted on to *R. ponticum* are so influenced by the graft that grafted plants are hardier than those on their own roots. We have seen *R. x loderi* quoted as a case in point. They say that in eastern districts of England and Scotland a grafted plant will flower more freely and will be more frost resistant ; but we cannot confirm that by personal experience.

It has definitely been proved, however, that a hybrid, one of whose parents is not a strong rooting plant, will be improved in growth and size by being grafted. Children of the great *R. lacteum*, one of the finest yellow-flowered species, are examples of this. For all its great beauty *R. lacteum* is neither a strong-growing nor a long-lived plant when grown on its own roots, and its progeny, such as R. Mariloo (*R. lacteum* x Dr Stocker), are no better.

One of the difficulties of grafting modern varieties lies in the fact that both stock and scion must be of the same diameter to make a perfect union. This means that large-leaved hybrids should always be grafted on to large-leaved seedlings. Thus a speeding up of the flowering of these large-leaved plants is almost impossible, unless the gardener has a surplus of any one species or hybrid of approximately the same size which could be used as stock plants.

We are not sure if top or renewal grafting has ever been tried in the case of rhododendrons. It might prove satisfactory with the new grafting technique that originated in the United States and has been improved in New Zealand. This consists of the usual saddle graft performed in the standard manner, but instead of being carried out in January or February it is done during summer when growth in both the stock and the scion is most active. No heat is required but a high humidity is essential. This, of course, is easily obtained when grafting on young stocks, as these can be placed in a closed frame for a month or six weeks, but it would not be so easily accomplished in the open.

Root grafting on *R. ponticum* is also practised, and is better than usual top grafting, as there is little or no production of suckers, but it is not often done in the nursery trade owing to the difficulty of obtaining satisfactory stocks in quantity, and because the union of the graft is hidden below the surface of the soil.

With azaleas grafting by amateurs is quite unnecessary. The deciduous species and varieties layer with great ease, while most evergreens strike quickly from cuttings. In addition, azaleas on the Continent are grafted on to *R. luteum*. While it is easy to distinguish *ponticum* suckers from most old and all new rhododendron hybrids, it is often very difficult to separate the suckers of *R. luteum* from the young growth of *mollis* azaleas.

Layering

Ground layering is the one method of propagation that has not altered throughout the years. Although slow it is eminently suited to the private garden with established plants. But to be successful one or two rules must be observed. The main one is that young wood must be used. It is no use thinking that by layering a long branch on the old wood as near the parent plant as possible a mature plant will root and a new plant will appear like magic. If such old wood roots at all, which is very unlikely, the rooting will take two or three times as long. In addition, such a branch if layered near the tips will probably have divided into multiple young shoots. If each of these is anchored in the soil, quite a number of layers will be produced.

The shoot must be securely anchored, and at the same time as acute a bend as possible must be made so that root formation will be stimulated by the contraction of the flow of sap. Soil can be built up above ground level in the moist conditions of the west, which makes the actual bending easier in the case of a plant with stiff branches, but in the drier east such a method would mean a longer time taken to root owing to the mounds drying out.

It is better to dig a narrow trench. Again the soil must not be too friable, as perfect drainage will mean drying out, nor must it be too solid, as that will not help root formation. We mix old potting soil in equal quantities with our rather

heavy loam. Another advantage of the trench is that when
the branch is laid in it, and the rooting soil tamped down,
the whole can be held in place by a piece of flat sandstone
or paving stone. The weight is sufficient to keep the branch
from springing up, and it also helps to keep the soil cool and
moist underneath. Pegging is sometimes necessary in the
case of a very springy branch, but where possible it is better
avoided.

You will sometimes be advised to cut a longitudinal slit
in the bottom of the shoot where it is buried and to rub in
a little rooting hormone. We have tested both with and
without these slits, and have found little difference.

Most of the larger species take about two years to root
from layers. In our drier east coast we have had to wait
three years with very dry summers. Under such conditions
layers may die, as drought may prevent the parent from
sending sap round the acute bend in the layer. We lost
a number in the dry autumn and early spring of 1952–3,
and again in 1955. It has now made us more careful about
watching not only the layer but the parent plant. A good
soaking may make all the difference between the life and
death of the layers. During the dull dark days of autumn
and winter we are not accustomed to associate drought conditions with a damp feeling in the air and frosty nights, but
they may exist at the roots and continue until there is a
heavy and continuous period of rain or a heavy snowfall.

There are plants so stiff in habit that ground layering
is not possible unless the parent is lifted and replanted on its
side, not a very becoming position for a plant in a private
garden. It is then that air layering is suggested. This we
have not done ourselves, but we do know first-hand that it
has been moderately successful. Although an air layer is

not a new device, yet it has been very much simplified by the use of a plastic covering. This has to be of a kind that retains moisture and yet is permeable to gases like oxygen and carbon dioxide. As far as we know tests that have been made show that the best is a Polythene film of a thickness of about four thousandths of an inch.

A longitudinal cut of about two inches is made through the bark of one-year-old wood and in this is rubbed a little rooting hormone. Then a handful of sphagnum moss, well moistened, but with any excess of moisture squeezed out, is packed round the cut and about an inch of stem on either side of the cut. This moss is tied into a ball with raffia. The plastic is wrapped round the moss with a big overlap so that no opening is left for evaporation of moisture, the overlap being at the bottom so that rain cannot seep in. The ends of the film round the stem are carefully wound round with adhesive insulating tape, the tape should be wound round the stem about an inch beyond the plastic at both ends so that no water can run down the stem.

The reason for this careful sealing is that it is just as important to keep rain-water from seeping in as it is to keep the moisture inside from evaporating. If excessive moisture gets inside, the sphagnum forms a soaking sponge in which no roots can form.

If carefully done, a plastic covering as described will remain in good condition for more than a year ; and roots apparently form more quickly in an aerial than in the ordinary layer on the ground. But more experimental work must be done in this country before such a method is counted a complete success. The difficulty is in starting the rooted layers into growth once they are severed from the parent.

In a mild and damp climate we have seen successful

layering in a wooden box with one end removed so as to allow the essential bend. The point is that ultimately the severed layer can be planted in its final position with the minimum of root disturbance.

Cuttings

It is with cuttings that there has been more advance. And yet has there? Thirty years ago L. B. Stewart, the great propagator at the Royal Botanic Garden, Edinburgh, produced roots on every kind and condition of rhododendron, even on leaves of *R. sinogrande*. But when showing anyone the results of his prowess, he usually ended by remarking that it was easy to make anything form roots, but a different matter to make the resultant roots form a plant. And this difficulty still exists today. It is quite an easy matter to make a whole batch of soft-wood cuttings of deciduous azaleas form roots, but it is often extremely difficult to make more than a very small percentage start into growth and form leaf-buds the following spring.

The frame equipment necessary for cuttings is the same as that for seed-sowing in heat, plus a cold frame facing north for the alpine species and hybrids, most of which dislike being forced to form roots in heat. Various mixtures are suggested as a rooting medium. We use one third finely sifted horticultural peat and two-thirds sharp and rather coarse sand, again with the proviso that it comes from a sand-pit, and is not dredged from salt water. Others use one-third vermiculite, acid or neutral grade, one-third sand and one-third peat. Others again have used pure vermiculite, but this presents a difficulty if you have cuttings of a number of different species and hybrids in the frame. Vermiculite is completely sterile and has no feeding value.

31

Thus when a cutting has rooted in vermiculite it must be removed promptly. This causes disturbance among the unrooted cuttings, which are much better left undisturbed for as long as possible, and extra labour is an almost daily examination. We from our personal experience prefer peat and sand to vermiculite.

In all cases the surface of the rooting medium should come to within a few inches of the glass so as to leave as little air space as possible. Larger cuttings are often inserted round the edge of a small earthenware pot, filled with the same mixture, and then the pot is sunk in the rooting medium in the frame. It sounds a redundant operation, but it does help with cuttings that are difficult to root.

It is only natural with a large genus like rhododendron when something or another is in flower for eight months in the year that it is quite impossible to go round a collection and take all the cuttings you want on the same day, or during the same week or during the same month. Mr F. E. W. Hanger put the matter in a nutshell in an excellent paper read before the Rhododendron Conference on 27 April 1949 when he said : 'The whole secret (if secret there be) of success is to remember that : (1) The larger the leaf and wood of the plant, the softer the cutting and the warmer the conditions needed. (2) The smaller the leaf and wood, the harder must be the wood of the cutting and the colder the conditions for rooting.'

Theoretically that means that if you want to take cuttings of a member of the *Grande* series you take them in July, and the dwarf *Lapponicum* series in December. In practice anything larger than the *Saluenense* and *Scabriolium* series are usually grown in heat. But the dwarfs are frequently rooted from cuttings taken in July and grown in heat or cold frame, equally as well as those taken in December and rooted in a cold frame. We prefer those taken in December, as the resultant plants are often sturdier, although the rooting naturally takes longer. Quickly rooted cuttings in heat in August have to be watched very carefully against drought and scorch during months when there are often extreme variations in temperature.

What is required is to see that the young wood is at the requisite degree of ripeness before the cuttings are taken. It does not really help to list the best time to take cuttings of various species or hybrids, as this depends so much on the season, and also on the part of the country in which the clonal plant is growing. To give a few examples ; during 1954, a frost-free spring, a wet summer and a sunless autumn, growth was early in starting and fairly early in ripening. We were successful with cuttings of Elizabeth taken in early September, *R. augustinii* and Blue Diamond at the very end of September, and most of the *Lapponicum* series in mid-December. There is no rule of thumb that can be given. The correct time only be learnt from experience ; and even then it is often guess work.

Cuttings are taken from this season's wood. A shoot is carefully pulled off with a heel of old wood. Wherever possible the cutting taken should be of short or medium length and not from long whippy growths, from the mistaken idea that they will give a larger plant in a shorter time. Side shoots are better than those from a main growing point. Cuttings with flower buds should always be avoided. Cuttings should not be taken in the middle of a hot day. The heel should be neatly trimmed, but never removed entirely if possible. An excess of foliage can be cut off, or several large leaves halved.

There are various growth substances, sometimes called hormones, which aid in the speedy and better formation of roots, once they have started to grow. It is not true that these growth substances will make roots grow where they would not otherwise appear. This rooting aid has been used for a number of years. It has lately been found that wounding of the stem of large cuttings before dipping them in the hormone is a further aid in some cases to more rapid callusing and root formation. A thin slice is cut off the outer bark, if possible exposing the cambium layer, but not cutting through it. While the wound is till moist, it is dipped in the hormone and inserted at once in the cutting frame. This system is used extensively in the United States for increasing the rooting of hardy hybrids.

We have used this procedure with a good many species and a few hybrids. With some it undoubtedly helps. With others it did no harm but the advantage was certainly not obvious. A good deal of detailed study requires to be done before definite rules can be laid down about the propagation of rhododendrons from cuttings. It is only natural that such wounding is impossible with the thin branchlets of dwarf rhododendrons. When dealing with a number of cuttings of the same species or hybrid it is better to insert them in blocks rather than in rows. Then, when one set of cuttings has rooted, they can be lifted with less disturbance to their neighbours.

Having inserted the cuttings in the heated frame, they are watered in, the frame closed and shaded and the thermostat set between 55° and 60°. Unless you are dealing with hard-wooded hybrids there is no point in having a higher temperature. The frame is left open for thirty to sixty minutes every morning to allow excessive condensation

Rhododendron fargesii

to disappear. The cuttings are then syringed again before closing and shading the frame.

In the cold frame the cuttings are inserted in the same way, but the frame is not left open daily, and it is watered as and when required to keep the rooting medium moist but not too wet. It does not help to forget the cold frame during winter, as cold weather may dry out the rooting medium quite as effectively as a series of hot days.

When cuttings are rooted, we pot them up singly in $2\frac{1}{2}$- or 3-inch pots in the same mixture in which we prick off seedlings. They are then kept in a greenhouse for a few weeks to settle down before being transferred to a cold house or frame. The object with freshly rooted cuttings is to keep them growing as much as possible.

The Species of Rhododendron in their series

THE cultivation of rhododendron species has been going on in the British Isles for more than two centuries. It might be imagined that the universal *R. ponticum* would have been the first introduction, but it was beaten by more than twenty-five years by an American rhododendron and an American azalea. A list of dates is tiresome, but so many gardeners look upon rhododendrons as plants of the Victorian era at the earliest that we give the introduction dates of a few.

The first to be introduced by more than seventy-five years was the European *R. hirsutum* in 1656. It is interesting to speculate why the commoner *R. ferrugineum* had to wait until 1752. Earlier in the eighteenth century plants began to come in from North America. The first appear to be the two azaleas, *R. viscosum* and *R. nudiflorum* in 1734, closely followed by *R. maximum* in 1736. It seems a little odd that two such common plants in the eastern seaboard as *R. catawbiense* and *R. calendulaceum* should have to wait until 1809 and 1806 respectively before being introduced. Meanwhile *R. ponticum* appeared in 1763, *R. luteum* (*Azalea pontica*) in 1793, *R. dauricum* in 1780 and *R. caucasicum* in 1803.

The first rhododendron from the Himalayas was *R. arboreum* in 1810 followed by *R. campanulatum* in 1825, but *R. barbatum*, *R. griffithianum* and *R. thomsonii* had to wait until 1849 when they were introduced by Sir William Hooker. The first introduction from Japan was *R. mucronatum* in 1819.

The first introductions from China, about the year 1808, were certainly garden forms of *R. simsii*. The first introduction of a recognised species was most probably *R. fortunei* in 1855, although there is a possibility that a Lieutenant Champion sent home seeds of *R. championae* to Kew a few years before. This, however, is a greenhouse rhododendron from Hong Kong and a plant of little importance.

Thus the introduction of species rhododendron into the British Isles began as a trickle, and continued with a few minor freshets until the end of the nineteenth century. Ernest Wilson started the first flood of importations in 1904, a flood that became almost unwieldy from 1909 onwards when Forrest, Kingdon-Ward, Rock and Farrer were collecting in China and its neighbouring districts. The floods began to recede by 1940 with the last expeditions of Ludlow and Sheriff. Since World War II there have only been two or three new species, introduced mostly from the Himalayas.

When it is realised that the 1952 edition of the *Rhododendron Handbook* listed more than 750 species, it will be seen how the systematic botanists have spread themselves. In addition more than 350 names have already been classed as synonyms. It was realised years ago that in order to avoid absolute chaos rhododendron species had to be classified in some form. Sir Isaac Bailey Balfour started this great work at the Royal Botanic Garden in Edinburgh, assisted by Mr H. F. Tagg, then followed by Sir William Wright Smith, Dr J. M. Cowan and Mr H. H. Davidian. It is to them that we must give thanks for producing some kind of order, a terrific task.

It is now generally realised that many rhododendrons cannot be tied down by definite characteristics into clearly defined species or even series. A general revision is under way, but it will take many years to accomplish. In the meantime we have to work with what already exists.

The following pages consist of short descriptions of some, but not all, of the worthwhile species for cultivation in gardens today with our opinions of their garden value, for what our opinions are worth. We happen to be species enthusiasts, partly from a genuine love of plants that have grown in the wilds and may take kindly to garden conditions, partly because we think that many hybrids are not improvements on their parents, and partly because the multiplication of hybrids *ad infinitum* is going to make the confusion worse rather than better, and make the choice of suitable plants for garden conditions even more difficult.

In most cases the plants mentioned are obtainable, at least from time to time. The difficulty usually lies in the *Grande* and *Falconeri* series which are extremely difficult to propagate by vegetative means. As some years elapse before a sizable plant is produced from seed, it is not everyone who is prepared to give up space and time in raising batches of young plants that may or may not be disposable.

The line drawings by Miss Margaret Stones illustrating all the important series depict a typical, but not necessarily the type, species in the series. In four series coloured plates take the place of line drawings.

Albiflorum series

This is a series with a solitary species, *R. albiflorum*, the Cascade rhododendron, which ranges from the Rocky Mountains and Vancouver Island through Washington to Oregon. It is peculiar in producing solitary flowers, about one inch in diameter, almost campanulate in shape with a conspicuously large calyx from lateral buds along the branch-

lets. The colour is white or creamy white, occasionally with
yellow or orange markings. The foliage is deciduous, about
two inches long, bright green above.

R. *albiflorum* forms thickets up to six feet in height, but
has always proved to be a very difficult plant in cultivation.
Some American authorities suggest that it possibly requires
the most acid conditions of any rhododendron in cultivation.
As in so many deciduous species the foliage is not striking,
but it colours well in autumn. In flower it is variable, but
Canadian friends tell us that the best forms are strikingly
beautiful, and that every effort should be made to experiment
so as to understand its horticultural requirements.

Anthopogon series

This series of small shrubs consists of species originally
included in three series, *Anthopogon, Cephalanthum* and *Fragrans*.
They are all small shrubs from one to four feet and varying
from compact to loose-growing shrubs with long young
growths. All have a terminal inflorescence, a compact
rounded cluster, not unlike the inflorescence of a daphne,
made up of small flowers with a narrow tube. All flower
in April/May. Some of the species are difficult to distinguish and tend to run one into the other. There could
be no better proof of this than the fact that no less than
twenty named species have lately been reduced and are now
classed as synonyms. While they can be classed as typical
rock-garden plants, most of them are not so hardy as other
dwarf species. They must have some shelter from cutting
winds, and in the south at least are the better for some shade.
On the east coast of Scotland we consider that R. *trichostomum*
and its varieties, which we think are possibly the best in the
series, are more plants for the milder west coast where the

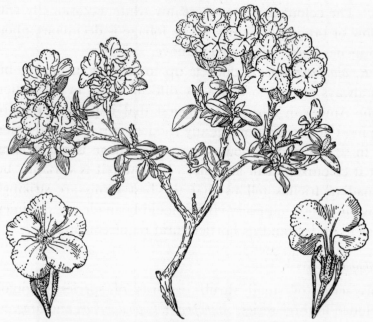

Anthopogon series : R. cephalanthum var. crebriflorum
(two-thirds natural size ; details × 1½)

conditions are moister and the soft young shoots are not so liable to frost damage.

The Himalayan *R. anthopogon* is one of the hardiest of the series. It grows 12–18 inches in height. The leaves are up to 1½ inches long by 1 inch wide, larger and broader than in others in the series. The flowers are white or pink, or yellow in the case of var. *haemonium*. *R. cephalanthum* is botanically very close to *R. anthopogon* but has persistent bud-scales. In cultivation it is usually taller-growing with longer shoots. The colour of the flowers varies from white to pink. Its form *crebriflorum* is a charming little plant.

R. primulaeflorum is an aggregate of a number of former species widely distributed from Kansu through Szechuan and Tibet south to Yunnan. Again it is so like *R. cephalanthum* in cultivation that if you have one, you will not want the other. One of the botanical differences is that in *R. primulae-florum* the bud-scales are deciduous.

R. sargentianum is a more spreading plant with short twiggy branches. The usual height is about 2 feet but it may reach 4 feet. The leaves are small, $\frac{1}{2}$ inch long and $\frac{1}{4}$ inch wide. The colour of the flowers is cream or yellow, sometimes pale and a little anaemic, but in the best forms a good primrose. It is quite hardy, and flowering in May escapes many spring frosts. It will also stand less shade. We consider it to be a first-class garden plant.

It is in *R. trichostomum* that we who garden on the east coast of Scotland sometimes suffer disappointment. It is a charming plant, though variable, taller, often reaching 4 feet, with some graceful arching branches as well as carrying the usual twiggy branchlets of the series. The foliage is longer, often up to $1\frac{1}{2}$ inches, and narrower than in the other species, and is not glabrous. The colour of the flowers is white or pink or rose. We once had a lovely salmon-pink form with almost grey foliage, but it was always inclined to be tender, and it finally disappeared during the war years. But for anyone who gardens in a soft climate like that of Cornwall, or the west of Scotland, almost any form of *R. trichostomum* is an essential plant ; but in colder districts one may expect damage if the frost comes during May, as growth comes early.

Arboreum series : Arboreum subseries

As one of the first rhododendrons to be introduced into the British Isles from the east *R. arboreum* was widely planted, particularly in south-west England and west Scotland. After all these years it still remains a magnificent plant when seen

Arboreum series : Arboreum subseries, R. arboreum
(*half natural size*)

at its best ; tree-like with a thick reddish trunk, handsome
foliage of a good green above and a white to fawn indumentum below, and very free-flowering with its upstanding
round and tightly packed trusses of many flowers, varying
from white through shades of pink to a rich blood-red. We
have seen many trees in Cornwall and in west Scotland with
trunks more than one foot in diameter four feet above the
ground. There are trees at Stonefield in Argyll almost
forty feet high and with trunks more than two feet in diameter, but they are exceptional.

It is only fair to point out its drawbacks ; its habit of very
early flowering, and the fact that many of the plants alive
today are seedlings of plants from the original importations,

and as such are often hybrids with *R. maximum* or *R. catawbiense* or *R. ponticum* that in the old days were planted alongside. This cross pollination has made their progeny considerably hardier. Whereas the true blood-red as seen at Caerhays Castle and other old Cornish gardens is undoubtedly a very tender rhododendron, as is its close cousin of almost the same colour, the Chinese *R. delavayi*. Some of those old hybrids, which are not so very different from the true species, are surprisingly hardy. There is a lovely tree more than twenty feet high at Balbirnie in Fife, a cold area, that is only one degree paler than the true blood-red *R. arboreum*. At Balbirnie that is the nearest approach to the true species. There are many others, all of them about a hundred years old, which show more clearly the admixture of foreign blood.

A number of the old plants on the west coast of Scotland originated at Stonefield at the mouth of Loch Fyne. Hooker sent some seed of his original introduction. These grew and flourished. Self-sown seedlings sprang up which were distributed far and wide.

R. arboreum and its alliance is the most widely spread of all rhododendrons, ranging from Nepal and the Himalayas, through Manipur to China, then to Ceylon and south India. Probably the hardiest form is the variety *album* which comes from a high elevation in Nepal.

For beauty of foliage *R. zeylanicum* from Ceylon must take pride of place. Its foliage is very dark green, more oval and strongly bullate, with rich pink flowers ; but it is only hardy in the extreme west.

It is said that another species, *R. niveum*, also forms a tree in the wild state. In cultivation we have never seen it completely dendriform, but as a large bush. It is always smaller than *R. arboreum*, but is a much hardier plant. It has never been really popular, as its colour is sometimes a muddy purple. Even in its best forms it is a difficult plant to place, although its dull purple flowers go well with its own foliage, dark green above and whitish beneath with a felted tomentum. Yet we have seen specimens growing as far apart as Inverewe in Ross-shire and Tower Court at Ascot that anyone would be proud to possess.

There is another species *R. silvaticum*, which at the time of writing is still included in the *Arboreum* series, although it is so like another species, *R. lanigerum* which is included in the *Falconeri* series, that it is impossible in cultivation to tell them apart at first glance. *R. silvaticum* forms a large bush with foliage like that of *R. arboreum*, but the indumentum of the young leaves is a clear white turning to grey as they age. The colour of the flowers varies from pink through red to a dark reddish-purple. One peculiar feature is the great size of the flower buds during winter. They seem to swell before the end of the year. As a bush it is quite hardy, but it flowers a little too early to escape spring frosts, and the flower-buds will not stand severe frost without serious damage. During the winter of 1954–5 a group of plants set with many hundreds of flower-buds had every one destroyed when the temperature dropped below 12° Fahr.

Arboreum series : Argyrophyllum subseries

There are a number of species in this subseries, some of which will certainly be reduced in time. With the exception of one, *R. insigne*, while pretty they are not wildly exciting, and most of them are too slow in coming into flower. They are, how-ever, all very hardy. Throughout the series the plants are more bushy and less tree-like, and the flower trusses are far looser than in plants of the *Arboreum* subseries. *R. argyro-*

phyllum has trusses of small pink bells, charming when in full flower, but fifteen years is a long time to have to wait to see this. In its best form, as at Glenarn in Dunbartonshire, it is particularly attractive. *R. floribundum* in its good forms is a rich purple, but too often it is a hot magenta. *R. ririei* is not of great value, although its red buds opening to dull purple flowers are pretty, but it is early flowering during February and March and takes years and years to flower. On the other hand *R. thayerianum*, a Wilson plant from western Szechuan, is, we think, valuable. It is one of the latest of all rhododendrons to flower, and never comes out before the end of June. It has long, narrow dark-green leathery leaves with a thin brown indumentum, and small trusses of little pink or flushed white bells. We have seen several plants that seem to be very regular in quality. We are surprised that it has not been used more often as a parent of cast-iron hardy hybrids with neat trusses. Such hybrids might be useful for the cold New England climate.

R. insigne, another Wilson plant, is certainly the best of the subseries. It is a much more spreading shrub, slow growing, with long-pointed leaves, 4 inches long by $1\frac{1}{2}$ inches wide, with a curious indumentum with almost a coppery sheen. The flowers are carried in a loose truss, in late May or June, and are a clear pink with crimson spots inside. We have a plant with a noticeably darker rose-coloured line down the outside of the petals, giving a most striking effect. Again it suffers from the time it takes to flower, but in this case it is well worth waiting for. With us, though now twenty years old, it never misses a year, and is never frosted. We place it among our twelve best rhododendrons.

Auriculatum series

This series has only two species, but both are important, *R. auriculatum* and *R. griersonianum*, and both are unlike any other rhododendron. While they have certain characteristics the same, such as very long and similar-textured foliage and flower-buds with particularly long bud scales, no-one is very happy at including them together in a series ; but there is nowhere else to put them.

R. auriculatum makes a large shrub, often flat-topped. The foliage buds are sticky when opening, and the pale-green young foliage is rather floppy, up to 12 inches long and 4 inches wide. The flowers are large and funnel-shaped, 4 inches long, in a loose truss, white with a greenish tinge at the base of the corolla ; and they are very sweetly scented.

It is among the latest rhododendrons to flower ; even in the west of England the flowers do not appear before the very end of July or early August. The young growth appears immediately after the flowers. While absolutely hardy, this late growth is a great drawback in the north and east. We in Perthshire find it completely useless, as it never ripens its wood enough to set flower buds. In addition, it requires a hot and damp August and September if it is to produce full-sized leaves, a greater heat than we can give it, with the result that much of its foliage with us is only half-size. If we lived on the west or south, we would never be without *R. auriculatum*. As it is, we cannot call it a useful plant.

On the other hand we do not understand the very general insistence in England that *R. griersonianum* is not really hardy. This is probably the most important rhododendron species in England today, not only for its own very real loveliness, but also because it has proved to be one of the best parents. Its

Auriculatum series : R. griersonianum
(*two-thirds natural size*)

named progeny are over a hundred, and include such great hybrids as Azor, Elizabeth, Fabia, Tally Ho, Romany Chai, F. C. Puddle, Matador, and that very remarkable plant Grierdal, the only hybrid that is definitely known to be a cross between a lepidote and an elepidote rhododendron.

It forms rather a straggly bush up to seven feet in height with long narrow dull-green leaves and a buff indumentum. The loose truss of five to twelve flowers is of that peculiar geranium-red that no other rhododendron species possesses. Frequently it has been said in the south that it has been killed to the ground in the winters of 1926–7 and 1939–40. As it flowers with us in June and July and produces its young growth in July and August, anyone would imagine that it

47

would suffer in the same way as *R. auriculatum*, but we find that once it starts to grow it grows rapidly and matures quickly. We have never had either young or old wood damaged, even in our particularly hard winters of 1946–7 and 1954–5. And this does not apply to only one or two plants, as we have almost a dozen in different positions, and they are all doing well. We have stressed this hardiness on the east coast of Scotland, as so many people who have written about rhododendrons have followed each other in claiming its tenderness.

Barbatum series

All the members of this series are more or less bristly, and in the *Barbatum* and *Crinigerum* subseries the relationship with *R. arboreum* is very marked both in habit and in the compact truss.

Barbatum series : Barbatum subseries

R. barbatum itself is one of the finest blood-red flowered rhododendrons ; in fact there are few species which conform to such a regular high standard. It is tree-like with handsome brown bark, while the foliage is striking owing to the very deeply impressed veins. The blood-red colour is quite pure with no hint of blue in it. The trusses are like those of *R. arboreum* in their light compact shape, but they are smaller.

While absolutely hardy, it flowers too early, in March, for it to be a perfect plant for northern gardens. It is quite bud-hardy, but naturally the opened flowers are cut by several degrees of frost. Thus it is seen at its best in the milder west and south. There is, however, a very close relative, *R. smithii*, slightly more hairy but with similar flowers that are produced a fortnight later. And this often makes all the difference. The leaves of *R. smithii* are also a much darker green. We have grown it for years and find it very satisfactory although it never carries a great crop of flowers.

Barbatum series : Crinigerum subseries

R. crinigerum is an extremely variable plant with one good point in its favour, that it flowers at an early age, while under three feet high, and so no-one has to wait long to see whether it is a good or poor form. It has long, narrow dark-green leaves up to six inches long and a thick tawny indumentum. We have seen some charming forms with flowers of a clear pale pink ; but it is only fair to say that we have seen horrors. It is a plant to see in flower before acquiring it.

Barbatum series : Glischrum subseries

R. glischrum itself is a plant unfortunate in its colour, but of good sturdy habit that will form a small tree and very handsome hairy foliage of a medium green and oblanceolate in shape, up to ten inches long. In its best forms it also possesses a handsome open truss of large flowers. It can be a deep rose with a deep crimson blotch at the base ; it can also be, and often is, a virulent magenta, only fit for the rubbish heap. It flowers at the end of May, or in June in the north. Having weeded out all our poorer forms, we like the few plants that we have left. We are careful to plant nothing near them that flowers at the same time.

It has a close relative, *R. glischroides*, a very rare plant that is highly spoken of. In addition to the usual bristles its veins are covered with fine white hairs, and the colour of the flowers is white flushed with rose, and a deep crimson blotch.

49

Another relation is *R. habrotrichum* that we like very much. It is even more bristly, and the bristles have a red sheen that is very attractive. The leaves are more oval and wider. The colour of *R. habrotrichum* also varies from an almost white to a deep rose. Our form happens to be almost rose-purple, again with the conspicuous crimson blotch. It flowers earlier than *R. glischrum* ; with us about mid-May.

Barbatum series : Maculiferum subseries

In this the plants are less tree-like and more bush-like, the leaves are smaller and the trusses are definitely more lax than in the *Barbatum* subseries. Some growers like *R. maculiferum* itself, a very hardy plant, for the striking contrast between the white flowers and the deep black-purple blotch at the base of the corolla, but we think the contrast a little too severe.

The real gem in this subseries is *R. strigillosum*, one of the best early reds. It forms a large many-branched bush up to 10 feet high and as much through. The foliage is almost as hairy as *R. barbatum* itself, oblanceolate, up to 7 inches long and $2\frac{1}{2}$ inches wide. The scarlet-crimson is almost, but not quite, as brilliant as that of *R. barbatum*, but the trusses are much looser and the individual flowers a little larger. Although it flowers early in March, the flowers will stand two or three degrees of frost, and no amount of cold will damage the unopened flower buds. We consider it an excellent plant for the east coast, as it is very free-flowering, although naturally you run a risk with all March-flowering plants. The young growth does not start till May, and even if it is cut it is at once replaced. In its best form we place it among the twelve best large-bush rhododendrons.

There are a number of others in the series, like *R. pachy-*

Barbatum series : Maculiferum subseries, R. strigillosum
(*two-thirds natural size*)

trichum and *R. monosematum*, which are sometimes listed but are not worth growing, and one, *R. pseudochrysanthum*, from Formosa, that is well worth growing and very rarely listed. We have only seen it once, but thought it a charming plant with pale-pink flowers richly dotted inside with crimson. It was in flower in April. We have not heard of its growing successfully in colder districts, but it would be well worth testing.

Boothii series

This series consists of three subseries, not entirely happily placed in one series, as the differences and relationships are more technical and not easily recognisable. The corolla is usually campanulate and the stamens are usually shorter than the corolla.

Boothii Series : Boothii subseries

Shrubs of various sizes with stiff branchlets, usually bristly, with campanulate flowers with very short flower stalks. In all species the colour is a bright primrose or butter-yellow. Most of them are neat small bushes with dark shiny green leaves, with fairly close terminal trusses that show up well at the end of the branchlets. But they are all plants from fairly low altitudes on mountains that bear the full force of the monsoon, and they are not very hardy. On the east coast we cannot grow any of them satisfactorily outside, but they are much more successful in the west and south-west.

The least rare of the species in the subseries is *R. sulfureum* which has been introduced under several names on many occasions, among them *R. theiochroum*, *R. cerinum* and *R. commodum*. It is two to four feet in height and as much through, although in the wild state it is often found as an epiphyte and is much more straggly. Four to eight flowers of a bright sulphur-yellow, not quite one inch across, are produced in a tight truss. We have seen excellent plants in the west and in Ireland but never in the east. There its place can be taken by its hybrid Yellowhammer which is a hardier plant.

Another member sometimes seen is *R. chrysodoron*, with larger flowers, three to six in a truss, of an even brighter yellow. It is even more tender.

Boothii Series : Megeratum subseries

This contains two most attractive shrublets that when mature vary between one and two feet in height and may be one yard or more across. They are stiffly branched, and often free-flowering. With their rounded hairy leaves, half to one inch long and about half an inch wide, and flat-faced flowers, usually carried singly or two together, they are neat. Their only fault is that they are early flowering and so are often cut. In *R. megeratum* the leaves are as a rule smaller than those of *R. leucaspis*, and the undersurface of the leaves is considerably more glaucous than in the latter. *R. megeratum* is also the more compact plant when grown outside. But *R. megeratum* always has flowers of a clear yellow, while in *R. leucaspis* the colour is invariably white.

In any garden that escapes much of the early spring frost these are both essential plants. *R. leucaspis* is not particular about soil, but *R. megeratum* does prefer one that is as peaty as possible if it is to flower freely.

Boothii series : Tephropeplum subseries

Much the showiest of the entire series is *R. tephropeplum* in its best forms. This forms a neat shrub two to four feet in height and more lax in habit, with longer narrower and more pointed leaves very variable in size, and a laxer truss of three to nine flowers on longer leaf-stalks of that shape called tubular-campanulate. The colour varies from blush white through pink to a rich rose. We like in particular the form that is almost a pure crushed strawberry. As it is very free-flowering the effect in full flower is delightful. It is quite hardy in a situation sheltered from cold draughts, but it should never be planted in a frost pocket, as we find the opening buds inclined to be frost-tender during late April frost.

The other important species in this subseries is *R. xantho-stephanum*, which used to be called *R. aureum*. It is much like

Boothii series : Tephropeplum subseries, R. tephropeplum
(*two-thirds natural size*)

R. tephropeplum in habit, but the colour of the flowers varies from creamy yellow to bright yellow. But it does differ in hardiness. *R. xanthostephanum* must be classed as a more tender rhododendron in the east and north, although it flowers at the same time as or even a little later than *R. tephropeplum*. We have grown it for a number of years, and have had to class it among those rhododendrons in which the unopened buds are frosted by more than twelve degrees of frost.

Camelliaeflorum series

R. camelliaeflorum is an old Himalayan species, usually found in nature growing as an epiphyte. It has been in cultivation for many years as a rare plant in greenhouses and occasionally outside in the extreme west. In growth and foliage it is reminiscent of many plants in the *Maddenii series*, but the flowers have a very short and very broad tube, and, indeed, look rather like a small camellia flower. The colour is white flushed with pink.

As several re-introductions of this interesting plant have been made lately it may become more plentiful. It is a good plant for a cool greenhouse.

Campanulatum series

This series is confined to the Himalayas. It is possibly nearest to the *Arboreum* series, but the leaves of all the species in the *Campanulatum* series tend to be rounded at both ends. The typical species, *R. campanulatum*, was one of the first to be introduced into the British Isles from India. It forms a large shrub with spreading branches, and is rarely tree-like. The leaves are dark, glossy green above, with a fawn or dirty brown indumentum below. The truss is fairly loose with about eight flowers, varying in colour from white, through pale and deeper rose to lavender-purple, often with deeper-coloured spots.

It is obvious with such a variable plant that there must be good and less good forms. In flower the best bluish form is certainly that raised at Knaphill and called var. Knaphill, with flowers of a rich lavender-blue, while in foliage much the best is that called var. *aeruginosum*, where the young foliage has a lovely blue metallic sheen. Even when mature the foliage is quite distinct. A third close relative is *R. wallichii* with less indumentum of a dirty rusty colour and almost magenta-mauve flowers. We would not grow it for preference.

R. campanulatum is certainly the hardiest tall-growing

Campanulatum series : R. campanulatum
(*two-thirds natural size*)

species from the East. Many old gardens throughout the
country have large specimens or clumps growing in almost
full sun and full of health, although they must be over a
hundred years old. As the result of more striking introductions from China its popularity has waned to a certain
extent, but for hardiness and good temper it should still have
its place in any collection of rhododendrons, particularly in
its forms Knaphill and *aeruginosum*. As it is such a variable
plant it should not be grown from seed.

R. fulgens is nearer *R. arboreum* in the shape of its tight
truss, although smaller, but in foliage and general appearance
it is nearer *R. campanulatum*. The colour is a rich crimson,
but unfortunately it flowers early in March and in conse-

quence is of little use in colder districts. As a plant it is quite hardy, and we grew it for a number of years, but when it was smashed by a fallen tree we did not bother to replace it. It is also very slow growing.

R. lanatum, very densely woolly with almost the deepest rust-coloured indumentum of any rhododendron, has a looser truss of pale-yellow flowers spotted with deep crimson. It sounds a little more attractive than it generally is in cultivation, as it is rarely a happy plant and is almost always shy to flower, although it flowers in April and May. We have never seen a plant that could be called a real success. However there have been several fresh introductions lately, and some of them may prove more amenable in cultivation. A well-grown and free-flowering form would be first class.

Campylogynum series

At one time or another a dozen or so names have been included in this series, but a detailed examination of all material has shown that the differences are so slight and the forms run so much, one into another, that it is now reduced to a monotypic series with one species, *R. campylogynum*, and several forms which differ only slightly from the type species.

It is the only rhododendron with nodding campanulate flowers like little thimbles, one to three carried on long pedicels. The habit is dwarf and spreading, with short branchlets and obovate leaves, dark green and highly polished, on the upper surface. The various forms differ in size. At the smaller extreme is the form that used to be called *R. myrtilloides*, and is now called var. *myrtilloides*. This is spreading and rarely exceeds one foot in height, with flowers under half an inch in length. At the other extreme is var. *cremastum* with paler and larger leaves, reaching two or more feet in height, and

Campylogynum series : R. campylogynum
(*two-thirds natural size*)

flowers a little over half an inch in length. Many years ago
J. C. Williams gave us an original plant from Caerhays,
and in due course in half-shade it grew to more than three feet
before it passed away from old age. Var. *charopoeum* is more
spreading, with the largest flowers, sometimes one inch in
length, as are the leaves. *R. campylogynum* itself is almost the
half-way house between its other varieties. In all of them
the colour of the flowers may vary from an almost salmon-pink,
through crushed strawberry, through purple with a bluish
bloom to an almost black-purple. Examples have also been
known of a greenish-yellow, but they are not attractive. The
paler-coloured forms are the most striking, that of crushed
strawberry being very pretty.

This is one of the best and most easily grown of all dwarf species. It should not be grown in too much shade, as it tends to become straggly. It is better to give individual plants plenty of room, as they make shapely and compact bushlets, too much so to plant too close together. As it flowers in May, there is little danger of frost.

Camtschaticum series

This also has one species, *R. camtschaticum,* in cultivation. It is also unique among rhododendrons as it flowers on the young wood. With its habitat in one of the coldest parts of the world it is surprising that it tolerates garden conditions in any form, but for many years it has flourished at the Royal Botanic Garden, Edinburgh, creeping along a high ridge at the top of the rock garden.

It is a most attractive plant, deciduous, with hairy spoon-shaped pale-green leaves. It never reaches more than six inches, following the contours of the ground and layering itself as it goes. The solitary flowers are large for the plant, five-lobed about one inch broad, rose-purple with the tube on the lower side split almost to the base, another unique diagnostic mark. They appear at the end of May or June.

This is one of the few rhododendrons that grows much better in the coldest part of the east coast than in the south. Wherever it is planted, it must be given full exposure to wind and sun with perfect drainage, but where it can be watered during the growing season. Thus it is not an easy plant, nor can it be suited in many gardens, but it is worth trying, as a large mat in full flower is most attractive.

Carolinianum series

This series consists of three closely related species from the eastern United States. They are all from 4–6 feet in height, with very thin branches and branchlets, giving a loose effect to the plants. The leaves are elliptic, 2–3 inches long and 1–1½ inches wide dull, green above and faintly brown beneath from scales. The flowers are usually rose-coloured, sometimes white, carried in loose trusses. They are all about 1 inch long. In cultivation we can see little difference between *R. carolinianum* and *R. chapmanii*, except that the latter coming from west Florida is only hardy in the south and west, whereas *R. carolinianum*, flowering in May and June and standing the rigours of the New England climate is cast-iron hardy.

It is really a much better plant than most gardeners imagine for cold gardens, and should be more often grown. It grows fairly quickly and flowers at a comparatively young stage. It is graceful and charming in flower, particularly the white form, but it is best grown in groups and not as single plants. It is sometimes listed in catalogues as *R. punctatum*.

Cinnabarinum series

This is another series that is confined to the eastern Himalayas and does not spread into China. The type species, *R. cinnabarinum*, in several of its forms has been in cultivation for more than a hundred years, and of hardy lepidote rhododendrons, they are almost the most beautiful. In its various forms it is a shrub from four to eight or ten feet high with fairly stiff branches ; thus it often has a rounded top. The foliage is obovate and glaucous, so much so that it

Cinnabarinum series : R. cinnabarinum var. roylei
(*two-thirds natural size*)

has a distinct bluish tint. The leaves are variable in size, up to 3 inches long, obovate, with a rounded mucronate apex. The small truss has four to five tubular flowers.

Of the older varieties the favourite has undoubtedly been var. *roylei* with cinnabar-red flowers, something like a Lapageria, a charming good-natured plant where the colour of the flowers blends in with that of the foliage. It is the tallest growing of the varieties and will reach eight feet or a little more. Another old variety is called *blandfordiaeflorum*, with a curious blend of red on the outside of the corolla and yellow, often greenish, within.

In the 1930's two fresh introductions were made by Ludlow and Sherriff. These plants are not always so tall growing, and so far usually appear to be forming rounded bushes about four to five feet each way. The leaves are slightly smaller, nor are they so glaucous. The flowers vary in colour from a clear yellow, through buff and orange, to apricot, orange-pink and mauve-pink. Almost all are attractive and quite free-flowering at a comparatively early age.

Much rarer and nearer to var. *roylei* is a purple-flowered form, called var. *purpurellum*, a rich plum-purple, but not so attractive to our eyes as var. *roylei*. There is still another called var. *pallidum*, a dull mauve-pink that is not nearly so good.

As all forms flower towards the end of April and during May and in the first half of June, they are rarely damaged by a very late frost. We grow them in half-shade. Our oldest plant flowers every year, and every second year flowers with great freedom. So long as it can be sheltered from wind and is not too dry, it is as good-tempered as any rhododendron species. We would certainly include var. *roylei* among twelve essential species of medium height for our Scottish east coast gardens. In some gardens in the south of England some forms are not so free-flowering.

R. concatenans is closely allied, but the flowers are a good deal more bell-shaped and apricot in colour faintly tinged on the outside with purple, and sometimes conspicuously veined. It is almost, but not quite, as hardy. We do not like the colour combination so well as the better forms of the Ludlow and Sheriff introductions of *R. cinnabarinum*.

There is another species, *R. xanthocodon*, which up to now has been included in the *Triflorum* series, but which has now been transferred to the *Cinnabarinum* series, and may only be another variety of *R. cinnabarinum* itself. It is said ultimately to grow to a small tree fifteen to twenty feet high. It has paler green foliage and waxy pale yellow flowers more campanulate in shape. It has flowered freely in gardens in the south, but may not be quite so hardy. It requires shelter even in southern gardens.

The last species in cultivation is *R. keysii*, a queer plant, inclined to be leggy, with light green leaves, 3–4 inches long and 1 inch wide, densely scaly above and below. It has completely tubular flowers ¾ inch long, orange-red tipped with yellow. Unfortunately it is a tender plant, not for the colder parts of the country, although it flowers in June. If you like the combination of red and yellow, a better plant is the hybrid between *R. keysii* and *R. cinnabarinum*, called Cinnkeys.

Dauricum series

There are two species in this deciduous or semi-deciduous series, which would probably be classed as Azalea if it were not for the presence of scales which are always absent in azaleas. They are both rather straggling shrubs up to eight feet with comparatively few branchlets.

In *R. dauricum* there are two forms, one deciduous, the other, var. *sempervirens*, evergreen, but in both, the elliptic leaves, about 1 inch long, ½ inch wide, are rounded at both ends. The wide funnel-shaped flowers are more like those of an azalea. The colour is bright purplish-pink. In *R. dauricum* the flowers all come out at once in February and early March. It is absolutely hardy in both its forms, although the flowers may be cut. It is an excellent plant in all parts of the country, and flowers freely under all conditions, but in the north it is better grown in very little shade.

R. mucronulatum is deciduous with more acute foliage. The flowers are pale purple or rose, and are precocious

Dauricum series : R. mucronulatum
(*two-thirds natural size*)

instead of coming out all at once as in the case of *R. dauricum.*
They begin to appear in January and go on until March.
It also starts into growth early in spring, and is often cut, but
fresh growth is always produced. We grow *R. mucronulatum*
in half-shade, but we believe it would grow more tidily if it
was growing in almost full sun. It is useful in all gardens ;
if the first flowers are frosted, there are always more to
follow on.

Edgeworthii series

This is one of these small series that in the wild state grow
mostly as epiphytes. In addition it has the peculiar associa-
tion of both scales and woolly hairs on the undersurface of
the leaves.

R. edgeworthii, and its Chinese equivalent *R. bullatum*, can be treated as one and the same plant as they are so much alike in foliage and flower. Both have ovate, sharply pointed leaves, 2–5 inches long and about $1\frac{1}{2}$–2 inches wide, very woolly below and very bullate and rough on the upper surface. Both have trusses of two to three broadly tubular flowers, white or pale pink, with a large calyx, and both are very sweetly scented. In cultivation they usually form rather straggling shrubs up to 6 feet. But in cultivation *R. edgeworthii* from the Himalayas is more tender than *R. bullatum* from Burma and China. Indeed the latter has a reputation for being a tender plant that is not entirely borne out in practice. It has grown for years successfully in a corner of the wild garden in the Royal Botanic Garden, Edinburgh, and in other gardens in colder parts of the country. But it must be completely sheltered from cold winds that will blast the buds as they open towards the end of April or early May. It should also be planted with a west exposure. There are two forms of *R. bullatum*, one with pure white flowers, the other with flowers distinctly pink towards the base.

R. pendulum, another Himalayan epiphyte is a much smaller shrub in cultivation, rarely exceeding two feet, with wide-open, short-tubed flowers of white, tinged inside with yellow. The leaves are rounder and not bullate like those of *R. edgeworthii*. They are very woolly. It has grown outside in the rock garden at Edinburgh for a number of years, but it is not wildly exciting.

R. seinghkuense received an Award of Merit in 1953. The habit and foliage is similar to that of *R. bullatum*, but the leaves are smaller. One or two flowers are produced in a small terminal truss, about $1\frac{1}{2}$ inches across, and are broadly bell-shaped, sulphur-yellow with brown anthers. They are more like those of some of the *Boothii* series. While an attractive little plant, it flowers so early that it should be grown in a cool house and not outside, unless in the extreme west.

Falconeri series

This is one of the two series of so-called big-leaved rhododendrons. The other, of course, is the *Grande* series, and from this the *Falconeri* series is distinguished by a kind of two-layered indumentum. The first consists of funnel-shaped hairs which disappear leaving a thin skin.

The Himalayan *R. falconeri* is certainly the best-known, large-leaved rhododendron in our gardens, as it has been in cultivation for more than a hundred years. In this country it may form a large shrub or a small tree twenty-five feet or so in height, always handsome because of its cinnamon-coloured old branches and flaking bark. The leaves are oblong-oval up to one foot in length and half as wide. The upper surface is a rich rough green with the veins deeply impressed. The under surface has a dense rust-coloured indumentum. The truss is round with twenty or more flowers, widely bell-shaped, creamy-white or yellowish with dark-purple blotches at the base. The lobes are eight to ten. *R. arizelum* is the Chinese equivalent, and is very similar except that the leaves are usually smaller and the colour of the flowers much more variable. They may be cream, or pale yellow, or pink, or rose, or a so-called red form that has appeared at Lochinch, near Stranraer, which is more of a deep rose. All these are attractive, but there are also some with muddy purplish colours that are not worth growing.

Both these species grow almost as well on the east as on

Rhododendron wardii

the west coast, although naturally the damper the climate the more luxuriant will be the foliage and the quicker the growth. They flower in April and May, and so may be cut by spring frosts, but the young foliage rarely appears until June and escapes any frost. They should be grown in thin woodland sheltered from strong winds, and they should be so planted that they are never crowded by other plants. They are quite handsome enough to stand on their own. *R. arizelum* in particular requires moisture during the growing season. If dry conditions exist, the foliage does not develop properly.

R. basilicum from Upper Burma and western Yunnan is easily distinguished from *R. arizelum* by the flattened winged petioles, while the indumentum is often paler. The flowers are usually cream-coloured with a dark-crimson blotch. This we find a more difficult plant, and much slower growing ; indeed, it is better left to those who can grow it in a milder and softer climate.

Still another close relative is *R. eximium*. This in turn can be distinguished by the rusty indumentum on the upper surface of the leaves that is persistent or semi-persistent until they are over a year old. The truss is a little smaller, and the colour is usually flesh-pink, cream or a not particularly attractive rose. It is very handsome when the young foliage is coming out. Although shapely it is never such a large plant as *R. falconeri*, though it is as hardy.

R. hodgsonii is another of the large-leaved species that grows well in colder districts, so long as it can be sheltered from wind. It is usually tree-form, or forms a very large shrub, with dark-green silvery leaves smoother than those of the previous species, and with a buff-grey indumentum below. The colour of the flowers is rose-mauve with a deeper blotch at the base. It is certainly long-lived and should be

Falconeri series : R. fictolacteum
(left, *one-third natural size* ; right, *one-sixth natural size*)

given plenty of room. A well-flowered plant is most attractive, but it is more easily tattered by wind than others in the series.

R. galactinum should not be bought unseen, as there are some very poor forms with muddy-purple flowers. But at its best it is an attractive shrub with dark-green glabrous leaves up to 7 inches long and 2½ inches wide, with a pale velvety indumentum. The best-coloured forms are a deep rose. It is quite hardy. Another species sometimes listed is *R. lanigerum*, but this is practically synonymous with *R. silvaticum* of the *Arboreum* series (p. 44).

Finally there is *R. fictolacteum*. This is a very variable plant. One of Forrest's early introductions has small leaves,

68

under six inches long with a buff indumentum. This has pure-white flowers, about twelve in a truss, with a moderate-sized crimson blotch. It forms a small tree about fifteen feet in height. At the other extreme is the form that is usually called *R. rex*, with more oval leaves up to twelve inches long, dark shining green, with a pale buff indumentum below. It has a large truss of twenty to thirty flowers, rose-coloured with a dark basal blotch and crimson spots. Between these two extremes lie a complete range of forms, so much alike, except in size, that they cannot be given varietal names that will stick. We find the small form by far the most free-flowering, but our largest plant, near *R. rex*, is most attractive in foliage and in flower. We have, however, an intermediate form, over thirty years old, with good foliage, but extremely shy-flowering. The best form is that introduced by Kingdon Ward under number K.W. 4509.

R. fictolacteum is said by some to be a better plant on our east coast than on the west. We find it very satisfactory in the two extreme forms, although flowering in April the flowers are sometimes cut. But growth comes late and escapes all frost. Like all this series it should be given plenty of room in which to expand, and should not be grown in too dense shade.

Ferrugineum series

The type, *R. ferrugineum*, the well-known plant from the European alps, is far too often ignored in gardens. It is a small shrub, often with leggy branches unless it is grown in full exposure. The leaves are oblanceolate, 1 to $1\frac{1}{2}$ inches long, and about $\frac{1}{2}$ inch broad, densely scaly below. The flowers are tubular, with loose scales but no hairs outside, and are carried in a loose terminal truss. The colour

Ferrugineum series : R. ferrugineum
(two-thirds natural size)

varies from pink to a rich rose-red, with occasional albino forms.

R. hirsutum is a close relative, but can be told from *R. ferrugineum* by the bristly hairs on the margins of the leaves, and the short hairs that fringe the corolla lobes. As a rule *R. hirsutum* grows as a more compact shrub. The third species, *R. kotschyi*, which is only found in Transylvania and Bulgaria, is smaller in every way, and the corolla has soft hairs both inside and out. The last is a rare plant in gardens.

The real difference between *R. ferrugineum* and *R. hirsutum* is that the latter is found on limestone, and can be grown in a moderately alkaline soil. Both are plants of great beauty. There is nothing quite like them among the Asiatic or American rhododendrons, as they are very twiggy, very leafy, and yet the flowers perch up well above the foliage in their racemose infloresences. While slow growing, they flower when quite small, and they are undoubtedly long-lived for a small rhododendron.

A natural hybrid is found in the Alps which is called *R. intermedium*. We imagine this to be the same as an old hybrid which is still sometimes listed by old-fashioned nursery-men as *R. wilsoni*. This is closer to *R. ferrugineum* than to *R. hirsutum*, but is a larger-growing and slightly larger-flowered plant. We have plants, 4 feet high and 5 feet in diameter, more than forty-five years old.

The whole of this series is very hardy. Flowers vary in colour and size, but as they are easily raised from cuttings, vegetative propagation of the best forms presents no difficulties. We repeat again that they are worthy of being grown in every rock garden, and should be far more often seen.

Fortunei series

This is one of the most important series, not only for the real beauty of many of its members, but also because a number of them are excellent parents, and from *fortunei* blood have come some of the finest of modern hybrids. As a rule the mature foliage of all members of the series is glabrous, usually with well-rounded ends. The flowers are usually funnel-campanulate and fleshy, with a very small calyx.

Fortunei series : Calophytum subseries

Only one of this subseries is in cultivation, the type, a large bush up to fifteen feet. It is an exception to the rule of the rounded ends in the foliage, as the large and long leaves are almost one foot in length and only two to three inches wide, tapering to a pointed end. The flowers are wide-open and bell-shaped, sometimes up to thirty in a loose truss with a very long rhachis. The colour is white or varying shades of pink, always with a dark-crimson blotch.

For the introduction of this handsome plant we have to thank E. H. Wilson who found it in north-western Szechuan ' extraordinarily abundant, trees forty to fifty feet tall and five to seven feet in girth, with handsome cinnamon-brown bark, covering many acres.'

Unfortunately in cultivation it does not grow larger than a big shrub, but with its rosettes of long-pointed leaves and large trusses, it is a most distinctive and handsome plant. We have found it quite hardy, but it is too early in flower with us, at the end of April, to escape all the spring frosts. Nor is it as free-flowering as farther south. Nevertheless we would never be without it. It is one of those shrubs that must be given plenty of room, as it grows as broad as it is high, and loses its character if it is one of a crowd.

Fortunei series : Davidii subseries

This is really a misnomer, as *R. davidii* is not in cultivation, and is not typical of the rest of the subseries. It might possibly be changed in time to *Sutchuenense subseries*. From a horticultural point of view it is rather a half-way house between the *Calophytum* subseries and the *Fortunei* subseries. It tends towards the narrower foliage of the former and the general appearance of the flowers of the latter, as they are not bell-shaped as in *R. calophytum*, nor do the trusses carry so many flowers. In *R. sutchuenense* the lobes are usually five or six, and we have a plant from Wilson's original intro- duction with seven lobes. The colour is usually rose-pink with no blotch but darker spots, while in the variety *geraldii* the colour is a little deeper and there is a more conspicuous basal blotch. The difference between them, however, is so small that the varietal name, *geraldii*, could well be dropped. There is another named species, *R. praevernum*, which is probably only another variety, as the only noticeable difference between it and *R. sutchuenense* is in the white or almost-white colour of the flowers, again with a deep-crimson basal blotch, and in the narrower and often longer leaves.

All three forms are worth growing. Their only fault is that they are a little early flowering. On the other hand they do not conform to any time-table : in a mild early spring they may start to open at the beginning of March in the south, but if the winter is prolonged they will show no colour until April. And the same applies with a time-lag farther north. The buds are completely hardy and the growth is rarely damaged. These large sturdy shrubs, with stiff branches, are like *R. calophytum* and must be given ample room.

R. planetum also belongs to this subseries. It is equally tall-growing, but the leaves are smaller and a paler green and do not form such obvious rosettes. The branches are not so stout, nor is the truss so compact. The colour is always a good clear pink without blotches or spots. Like the others it is a little early-flowering, and we have also found it slow to flower. While *R. planetum* is a pretty shrub, *R. fargesii*, which it superficially resembles, is probably a more reliable plant for the ordinary garden.

Fortunei series : Fortunei subseries
Botanically this subseries is quite distinct, as all the species in it have a style that is totally glandular, while other subseries have styles that are either glabrous or slightly glandular at their base. The *Fortunei* subseries consists of

stout shrubs with rather looser flower trusses. *R. fortunei* itself is a very rare plant only found in a few old rhododendron collections. It has been used extensively as a parent, and is an excellent one, but that very fact makes it important to see that a plant has been produced by vegetative means and not from seed, as the latter is almost certain to have been cross-pollinated with something near by. We have seen very, very few true plants. Although very hardy, there are better species in the same subseries.

R. decorum is probably the commonest species in the subseries and the most widespread, as it ranges from Szechuan through Yunnan to Upper Burma. As often happens, the eastern plants from Yunnan and Szechuan are the hardiest, although the smallest in flower, while the plants from the monsoon areas of Upper Burma are much more tender.

It forms an erect shrub up to eighteen feet, with stout branches and smooth wax-coated oblong-obovate leaves up to six inches long and three inches broad. The undersurface is a pale glaucous green. The truss is loose and carries eight to ten wide-open flowers always sweetly scented. The colour varies. Usually it is white, white flushed with pink, or pale pink, but we have an aberrant form with almost lemon-yellow flowers called Cox's Uranium Green. There is also another yellow relative, if not form, at present given specific rank under the name *R. chlorops*. This is yellow tinged with green in the centre, and with a purple blotch and spots.

R. decorum is a hardy species, excepting plants from Upper Burma and a large-leaved form from the Shweli-Salween divide in Yunnan. It is extremely free-flowering once it has reached flowering size. Although the Farrer form from Upper Burma has the largest flowers and leaves, it is definitely bud-tender and should be avoided except in the west. We find the forms introduced by Kingdon Ward good garden plants in every way. They do not flower until the very end of May and show great variation in shade with good large-sized flowers. As it is always inclined to be upright, it is one of the larger shrubs that can be grown several in a group. We actually grow them as a hedge which is quite satisfactory. The thick leaves will even stand a good deal of wind without damage.

R. diaprepes is even larger than the Burmese form of *R. decorum*. It is still later in flowering, and it suffers badly from bark-splitting. It is not a plant for colder districts, although it is a lovely plant in the south and west.

R. discolor is July-flowering with longer narrower leaves, but with the same sturdy stocky growth, reaching up to twenty feet. The individual flowers are very wide, up to five inches across, pale pink fading to white or white with a greenish centre, carrying about ten in a loose truss. While this is hardier than *R. diaprepes*, it also suffers from bark-splitting. If it is grown in colder districts it is essential that it should be sheltered from wind. Owing to its late flowering it is a valuable plant and worth trying in any sheltered situation. The farther north it is planted the less shade is necessary, so that the young wood may ripen.

The species that we like best in the series is *R. vernicosum* in its best form. This is like *R. decorum* except in the shape of the truss, which is more elongated so that the flowers face outwards and make an extremely elegant show. There are several geographical forms, var. *euanthum*, var. *rhantum* and so on. We may be lucky in the forms we grow, but we give it very high marks indeed. The colour is white or pale rose, usually with crimson markings. It flowers in April/May.

75

As it is a wide-spreading shrub of about eight feet or more, it is better grown as a specimen.

Fortunei series : Griffithianum subseries

This contains a solitary species, the lovely Himalayan *R. griffithianum*, parent of some of our finest hybrids, many of them hardy, although *R. griffithianum* itself is too tender for any except the most sheltered gardens in the west. In foliage and habit it is not unlike the larger members of the *Fortunei* subseries, with the addition of attractive brown-purple bark. The inflorescence is very different with only three to five flowers in the lax truss, and the individual flowers are widely campanulate, often five inches across. The colour is sometimes pure white, more often a faint pink. It is very sweetly scented, and is May-flowering. Where it can be grown there are few more beautiful shrubs, but even in the west it should have shelter from wind and a certain amount of shade. It is a real woodland plant.

Fortunei series : Orbiculare subseries

This also contains a solitary species in cultivation, and another one, *R. cardiobasis*, recently described but not yet introduced. *R. orbiculare* is a plant that has puzzled botanists for many years, as there are points of similarity between it and the *Fortunei* series and also with the *Thomsonii* series. In foliage and habit it is like some of the *Thomsonii* series, but the flower is in seven parts without pouched nectaries, those little cavities at the base of the corolla in *R. thomsonii*. Thus it is included in the *Fortunei* series. From a horticultural point of view it is possibly in the wrong series owing to its habit and general appearance.

R. orbiculare is always a rounded shrub, many branched

and with abundant foliage. The largest plants in cultivation are about seven feet tall and twice as much in diameter. The leaves are definitely orbicular, pale green, like larger examples of the foliage of *R. williamsianum*. The corolla is campanulate, always rose-coloured, and carried in trusses of seven to ten flowers. It is not scented.

This is one of the neatest habited of all rhododendrons, and must always be grown by itself. It is quite hardy, but flowering in April/May it may be caught by spring frosts. It is particularly attractive if planted where it can be seen from above. Conversely it should never be planted above a path. It should be grown in more sun than usual so as to make a compact plant. In shade it becomes leggy and loses much of its shapeliness.

Fortunei series : Oreodoxa subseries

There are at present four species in this subseries, all from Szechuan, Hupeh and Kansu, and all so closely allied that they could, from the garden point of view, be considered as one species with several varieties. The two most often listed are *R. fargesii* and *R. oreodoxa*, which mainly differ by the presence of glands on the ovary of the former, and by the narrower foliage of the latter.

They are tall shrubs up to eighteen feet, with rather stiff ascending branches with leaves up to five inches long and two inches wide. The truss consists of six to ten flowers, openly campanulate, and varying in colour from off-white to a deep rose (*R. fargesii*, coloured plate facing page 34). There are a number of geographical forms, such as *R. reginaldii* from Kansu, very similar in appearance but pale in colour and not nearly so free-flowering with us as plants from farther south in China. Although all the group flowers in March or early April, they will stand colder weather than most, and even if the buds are showing colour we have found that they will survive several degrees of frost. With these variations there are some that do not flower until they are at least half grown and others that will flower when only three or four feet tall, but with the exception of *R. reginaldii* we have found them extremely free-flowering once they are nearly mature. This takes a good deal out of the plants. If they are to remain healthy they should certainly be fed every year after flowering. Their foliage forms a good test of both cold and drought conditions, as it curls up if there are several degrees of frost or when the soil gets really dry, but it soon uncurls when conditions return to normal.

Fulvum series

This small series is near the *Campanulatum* series. There are now only two species in it, *R. fulvum* and *R. uvarifolium*, both of them very like *R. campanulatum* in habit, forming a small tree or large bush. *R. fulvum* has cinnamon-coloured to pale fawn indumentum made up of mop-shaped hairs, the only rhododendron with this peculiar structure. It has been introduced many times, and the size of the leaf and of the flower varies a great deal. The colour of the flowers also varies from white to rose, some with crimson spots and some without. But it is always a neat plant, and on the whole very free-flowering with numerous trusses of smallish flowers rather than a few trusses of more imposing flowers. It is a useful early-flowering species, usually opening with us about a week or ten days after *R. fargesii*. One point in its favour is that owing to its leathery leaves and smallish flowers it will stand up to a good deal of wind without damage. We had a ' blow-through ' near two large plants, and for several

Fulvum series : R. uvarifolium
(*half natural size*)

years they have been exposed to our north-east wind, a very cold one. Yet they have showed no damage nor has it reduced their free-flowering quality. The leaves of *R. fulvum* also curl up with the cold.

The other species, *R. uvarifolium*, which used to be known as *R. niphargum*, is included in the series with less obvious reasons, as the indumentum is white, thin and smooth, while the upper surface is dark shining green, different in appearance from that of *R. fulvum*. This also is a very variable plant. Good forms are handsome in foliage, lovely when the young leaves are coming out, with firm upstanding trusses of a silvery pink with a deep blotch that go well with the foliage. Others are shy to flower even when mature plants, with moderate trusses of an indeterminate pink or off-white. We have several forms, the best very good, although they come into flower at least a fortnight earlier than *R. fulvum*, the worst merely a useful foliage plant.

Glaucophyllum series

This is a series of small shrubs, rarely exceeding five feet. There are two subseries, *Glaucophyllum* and *Genestierianum*. The latter has only two species, with no pretence of hardiness and of almost no garden value. The *Glaucophyllum* subseries on the other hand has several worthwhile plants.

R. brachyanthum reaches 4–5 feet and is spreading. The leaves are usually oblong-elliptic, from 1½–3 inches long, and very glaucous below. The inflorescence is terminal, 5 to 10 flowered with long thin flower stalks. The corolla is 5-lobed, campanulate, barely 1 inch long. The colour is greenish-yellow, or pale yellow in var. *hypolepidotum*, the better form. This is quite a valuable late-flowering plant, as it does not flower until June. We find it quite hardy. If it has a fault, it is that the young growth sometimes precedes the flowers and tends to hide them.

R. charitopes we consider a more attractive plant. With us it grows to 5 feet with much wider leaves. The truss is terminal with 3 to 4 flowers ; the flowers are larger, about 1½ inches long and apple-blossom pink with darker markings. It normally flowers in late April and May, but we find that if the autumn is mild the flower-buds begin to swell and even to open, with the result that a number are frosted. But it is very free-flowering. It would be more popular if it were easier to propagate, as it is one of the most attractive of the late spring smaller shrubs.

The type species under the present rules of nomenclature

Glaucophyllum series : Glaucophyllum subseries, R. charitopes
(*two-thirds natural size*)

must be called *R. glaucophyllum* instead of *R. glaucum*. It is usually 1½ feet high and 2–3 feet in diameter, but occasionally we have seen a taller form of up to 4 feet. It has a very glaucous undersurface to the leaves. It is closely related to *R. charitopes*, but the flowers are more numerous in the truss and the colour is usually rose or pinkish-purple. It is a useful and hardy shrub that flowers in May.

R. *shweliense* is very close to *R. brachyanthum*, but with pink flowers tinged with yellow with spots on the three upper lobes. The outside of the corolla is scaly ; in *R. brachyanthum* it is not.

Finally there is *R. tsangpoense* with a close relative, *R. pruniflorum*, that only differs in the number of scales on the undersurface of the leaves. This rarely reaches more than four feet. While very like the others in general appearance the flowers carried, two to six in a truss, are more thimble-shaped, somewhat approaching those of *R. campylogynum*, but on the typical thin and long flower-stalks of the subseries. This is particularly so in the var. *curvistylum*, where the leaves are smaller as well as the flowers, while the colour is cherry-red, while in *R. tsangpoense* the colour varies from pink to violet. Although not very exciting, these are useful small shrubs as they are completely hardy and flower in May and June. The other species in the *Genestierianum* subseries is *R. micromeres*.

Grande series

This magnificent series shares with the *Falconeri* series the possession of the largest-leaved rhododendrons of our gardens ; indeed the leaves of the *Grande* series are by far the largest in the genus. They all come from moderately low altitudes in areas which bear the brunt of the south-west monsoon, with the consequence that although some of them may grow in the Home Counties and even survive in the east of Scotland, they all require the mildness and dampness of Cornwall or Ireland or the extreme west of Scotland, if they are to show anything of their true habit. We have grown *R. sinogrande* in several forms for many years in eastern Perthshire. Though the individual leaves are very nearly as large as those in the milder west, there is no real growth, and rarely signs of a flower. A comparative newcomer, *R. macabeanum*, may prove to be an exception, as it is putting on excellent growth as a young plant ; but time will tell.

R. giganteum, as its name implies, is the giant of the genus. In the wilds it has been found 90 feet in height

(left) R. *lysolepis*   *(top)* R. *intricatum*   *(right)* R. *chryseum*

with a trunk of 9 feet in circumference 7 feet above the ground. In cultivation it has flowered at Brodick in Arran, at Arduaine, south of Oban and at Mount Stewart in Northern Ireland, among other gardens, but it will always be a plant for the very mildest gardens in the British Isles with complete protection from wind, as it starts into growth very early in the year. The flowers are a deep rose-pink with a deeper blotch. With it must go *R. magnificum* and *R. protistum.* To begin with these were counted as different species owing to presence or absence of indumentum at the back of the leaves, but as similar variations have been found together on one plant, there is no need to separate them. *R. protistum* in the wilds has creamy-white flowers, but we are not certain if it has flowered in this country.

R. grande does not have the large elephant's ears of *R. sinogra.* In this the leaves are oblong-oblanceolate usually about eight to ten inches long and three to five wide with a silvery or pale tawny indumentum. The truss is large with about twenty bell-shaped flowers white or creamy white with a basal purple blotch.

As this is a plant of the Himalayan rain-forest, it is equally tender, but for those with a very mild garden it can be a lovely plant with the silvery undersurface of the leaves showing off the numerous flowers. There is a very fine specimen at Brodick, and we remember lovely plants in old Cornish gardens such as Penjerrick and Lanarth.

In *R. macabeanum* we have what is probably one of the most promising of the large-leaved rhododendrons for ordinary gardens. Its ultimate size is said to be a tree up to forty feet high in sheltered gardens on the warmer and damper west coast, but it is growing fairly rapidly even in drier parts of the country. While it is certainly growing to be a large plant,

Grande series : R. grande
(one-third natural size)

it tends to cover more ground than it is making height. Its leaves are more oval and not quite so large as those of *R. sinograude,* and they are of the same very dark, very shining green. The trusses are first class in shape with twenty to thirty flowers, and are more compact as the pedicels are not quite so long as they often are in *R. sinograude,* which sometimes makes the huge truss a little floppy. The colour is a pale to bright yellow. With its truss up to ten inches in diameter, it is undoubtedly the finest yellow-flowered rhododendron.

It also has the advantage of flowering at an earlier age than any others in the series. Indeed it is so free-flowering when approaching maturity that it is a plant that must be fed in order to keep up its strength. We have seen plants on the west coast with more than a hundred of these huge inflorescences out at the same time. It is certainly the first large-leaved rhododendron that we would suggest planting in any sheltered garden in almost any part of the country. It is listed as flowering in March, but most plants that we have seen do not open their flowers before the middle of April.

R. sinogrande has larger leaves than any other evergreen grown in the open in this country with the exception possibly of *Magnolia delavayi*. It forms a small tree up to thirty feet tall with leaves of varying size and shape. Some are almost completely oval, others taper rapidly towards their base ; some may be ten inches long, others up to eighteen inches or even more, but they are all glossy, dark green above with a rather shining grey indumentum below, whereas in *R. macabeanum* it is more woolly. The racemose truss of twenty flowers, as mentioned above, is inclined to be rather floppy, but the effect of this mass of large bell-shaped creamy-white flowers each with a crimson splash at their base is most striking.

R. sinogrande is a plant that flowers strictly according to size. While hardy, it starts into growth too late in drier and colder districts for it to make much growth, although the size of the leaves may be adequate. Thus we have plants over twenty-five years old, barely six feet in height with never a sign of a flower until this year, whereas in Cornwall or south-west Ireland or the extreme west of Scotland it may grow one foot or more a year and thus flower at a comparatively early age. It must be given plenty of room in which to expand, as a well-grown tree may cover eighteen feet ; nor is it a plant that will transplant well, unlike most rhododendrons, as it tends to send roots deep into the soil at an early age.

There are other members of this series in cultivation, of lesser importance, such as *R. praestans*, noticeable for the large wings on its petioles, with rose-magenta flowers ; *R. sidereum*, a very tender plant with narrower leaves, like those of *R. grande*, very silvery underneath, and with creamy-yellow flowers with a large crimson blotch ; finally there is *R. mollyanum*, a close relative of *R. sinogrande*, that has appeared in cultivation and flowered in a few gardens on the west coast of Scotland. In habit and foliage there is little difference between the two, but the colour of the flowers is a clear rose to a paler rose with a slightly bluish tinge, with a crimson blotch. This is still a very rare plant and has only recently been named. It was originally called *R. sinogrande* before it flowered under numbers KW 6261 and 6261A. It is possibly a little hardier than many members of the series.

Heliolepis series

From our point of view this is one of the most difficult series on which to base reasonable descriptions and a garden estimate. It is very close to the more important *Triflorum* series. In fact, unless one is constantly among them it is very difficult to tell them apart. In the *Heliolepis* series the leaves are thicker in texture and often more scaly, enough so to give the foliage an olive-brown tinge. Some are taller-growing.

Also there is no doubt that within the series, the named species are so closely allied that apart from differences in flower colour and time of flowering they are practically the same. From the fact that the chromosome numbers

Heliolepis series : R. desquamatum
(*two-thirds natural size*)

for the series are tetraploid, hexaploid and even one octoploid, it might be possible to guess that the series is still in a state of flux ; in other words that they are all natural hybrids.

The two most frequently seen are *R. rubiginosum* and *R. desquamatum*. Both are tall shrubs about 15 feet with aromatic oblong-elliptic foliage, about $3\frac{1}{2}$ inches long and $1\frac{1}{4}$ inches wide, and both carry small trusses of widely funnel-shaped flowers, about 1 to $1\frac{1}{2}$ inches long, rosy-mauve spotted with brown in the case of *R. rubiginosum*, mauve to pale or dark lavender, also sometimes spotted in *R. desquamatum*. The latter has been sent home by various collectors from different areas. Whether we are particularly lucky in having a hardy form or not, our experience differs from that at Exbury (Hampshire), where we have seen plants damaged by April frosts. But we have grown it for almost thirty years in Perthshire and have found it just as hardy as any other April-flowering rhododendron. The colour of the better form is either a pale or a dark lavender-mauve. Both *R. desquamatum* and *R. rubiginosum* are very free-flowering; the latter at its best a little later than the former.

Still later, June-flowering in the north, are *R. heliolepis* and *R. fumidum*. They are also smaller growing, with rather smaller flowers. The former is very variable in colour, the best forms being rose with darker spots, the latter almost a purple-violet. Both are useful in prolonging the flowering period. *R. brevistylum* is so close to *R. heliolepis* as to be synonymous.

Irroratum series

This is a shrubby series somewhere about half-way between the *Arboreum* and the *Fortunei* series. If there is indumentum it is often fugitive. The inflorescence is rounded but not in such tight trusses as in *R. arboreum*. There are two subseries, the *Irroratum* and the *Parishii*.

Irroratum series : Irroratum subseries

This consists of shrubs in which the leaf texture is not unlike that of *R. ponticum*. The shape is usually lanceolate with an acute apex. With a few exceptions gardeners in the colder districts would be better to leave this series alone, particularly those in the *Parishii* subseries. While the list of names in the *Irroratum* subseries is imposing, many are not in cultivation, and of those that are, while hardy in themselves as plants, almost all are flower-bud and leaf-bud tender.

Anything above ten or twelve degrees of frost will kill the unopened flower-bud even in the middle of winter.

For warm and sheltered gardens on the west there are some lovely species which might well be tried. Among them are *R. araiophyllum*, a very straggling shrub with cup-shaped flowers of good shape, pure white with a deep-crimson blotch and crimson spots ; *R. laxiflorum*, a larger-growing bush, must be one of the most beautiful pure-white rhododendrons in existence. We have seen it in Cornwall in April, with its ivory flowers showing up like ghosts among the rich green foliage. But alas ! it is a plant only for Cornwall or the south-west of Scotland.

R. irroratum itself is much hardier. It is a very variable plant, in some cases with such small trusses as to be unworthy of garden cultivation. In others the truss is more open, with larger flowers of palest pink or yellow suffused with pink and almost always spotted. For many years we have had several plants growing exposed to the north-west and in fairly dense shade. They are almost apricot in colour, and although flowering early in April often come through our cold springs unscathed.

One other plant has been placed in this subseries, the new *R. aberconwayi*. This is a small shrub three to eight feet high with extremely leathery and brittle leaves, rare in a rhododendron, and a racemose truss of saucer-shaped flowers that stare one straight in the face. The colour is white, or white faintly tinged with pink with a few crimson spots. This comes into flower late for the series, in May and June, and is proving not only very attractive but also hardy. While it grows slowly on the east coast, yet it flowers at a fairly early age and is a distinct acquisition to our gardens.

Irroratum series : Parishii subseries

This very tender subseries contains some magnificent species, almost all from the monsoon areas of Upper Burma and western Yunnan, and almost all with brilliant crimson or scarlet flowers. In all cases the leaves are longer, less pointed and much softer in texture than those in the *Irroratum* subseries. We have seen most of them in flower in Cornwall or the west coast of Scotland, although we have had no personal experience of growing them in our harder climate. They all flower fairly late in May or June except the finest of all *R. kyawi* which does not flower until August, and oddly enough is in consequence the most tender, as its growth never ripens until late autumn ; so it must be grown in a frost-free situation. Probably the hardiest is *R. eriogynum* which comes from farther east in Yunnan than the others and has a firmer textured foliage. Those who live in colder, but not the coldest, gardens can share in their beauty owing to the production of some first-class red-flowered hybrids, such as Fusilier and Grenadier from *R. elliottii* and Tally Ho from *R. eriogynum*.

There is one plant so far included in the subseries, but which has affinities with *R. neriiflorum*, called *R. venator*. This is a bushy plant that will ultimately reach about eight feet, with smaller and narrower leaves. The trusses carry only four to six tubular-campanulate flowers about two inches long, and fleshy in texture but of the same clear scarlet-crimson colour. This oddly enough is proving quite hardy in colder districts if grown in a sheltered situation. As it flowers in May or June it escapes most of the spring frosts, and yet it does not grow so late that its young wood is never ripened.

Although both are aberrant species, in *R. aberconwayi* and *R. venator* we have two lovely plants from a tender series that are worth trying in any except the very coldest gardens.

Lacteum series

This series which lies somewhere between the *Campanulatum* and *Taliense* series is known chiefly for its two yellow-flowered members *R. lacteum* and *R. wightii*. While the two tall-growing shrubs *R. beesianum* and *R. traillianum*, both with white or rose-coloured flowers and crimson markings, have been introduced a number of times and are to be found in many collections, yet they are of little beauty and importance. They are not likely to be propagated further, and they are best forgotten.

Not so *R. lacteum* and, to a lesser extent, *R. wightii*. Before the arrival of *R. macabeanum*, *R. lacteum* was certainly the finest yellow species. Indeed, for the symmetrical beauty of its large truss and clear yellow colour it is very doubtful if the best forms could be beaten by any rhododendron. It will ultimately reach a small tree or large bush of more than thirty feet, with thick leathery oblong-elliptic leaves up to eight inches long and three inches wide, with a cordate base. The undersurface is a dull fawn. The truss is large with twenty to thirty flowers, widely campanulate, about two inches long, off-white to a clear yellow and no spots.

But *R. lacteum* unfortunately is one of the worst-tempered rhododendrons in cultivation. It is quite hardy if well sheltered, but it grows slowly, is difficult and refuses to respond in most gardens, and, for a large rhododendron, is short-lived. And, oddly enough, it has proved to be a poor parent. Good plants are still to be found, mostly in western gardens. The best plants that we know personally are at Lochinch, near Stranraer in south-west Scotland.

R. wightii is similar but with rather narrower leaves, a looser truss, paler flowers with a blotch and heavily spotted with crimson. While an attractive plant, the looser truss and paler colour remove some of the character that is so noticeable in the case of *R. lacteum*. On the other hand it is not such a difficult plant to cope with. We have seen good plants growing as far apart as Suffolk and Morayshire.

Lapponicum series

There is probably no more universally grown group of rhododendrons than the dwarf *Lapponicum* series, as they can be grown in the smallest garden. Most of them make attractive bushlets at all seasons of the year, except possibly when there is hard frost and the leaves curl up and shrivel. But this does no harm, as they uncurl to their natural shape as soon as a thaw comes.

Most members of this dwarf series take the place of our heather in the more open moorlands of eastern Asia. Many of them form matted growths, and collectors such as Kingdon Ward and George Forrest have commented on the kaleidoscopic effect of seeing purple, deep blue, pink, yellow and white dwarfs all flowering in close proximity to each other. All members of the *Lapponicum* series are hardy, and many of them make excellent plants for the rock garden.

The danger in cultivation is that they grow out of character because of being too well treated. In the north almost full exposure can be given. In the south, where the summer sun heat may be a little too severe, a little shade should be given. In any case the shears should not be spared if the plants become too obviously drawn.

We shall begin with two large species which lie half-way between this series and the *Triflorum* series. Even if they should not be removed into the latter series, most rhododendron growers agree that at least they should be included in a separate subseries. They are *R. cuneatum* and *R. ravum.* Furthermore if you grow either the one or the other, there is no need to get the missing species, as they are so much alike as to be one and the same plant in gardens. The former was found by Forrest in 1906 and the latter in 1913, so presumably the name *R. cuneatum* may remain and *ravum* disappear.

They are rather widely spreading shrubs up to four or five feet, with short, thick, densely scaly branchlets. The leaves are elliptic, fully an inch long, densely scaly on both surfaces. The inflorescence is terminal with usually four widely funnel-shaped flowers one inch long. The colour is deep rose to a rich pink.

We consider them to be very good value. While they do not flower at such an early age as some of the dwarfs, yet when they do they flower with great freedom almost every year. They flower with us in May and towards the end of April farther south.

In the *Rhododendron Handbook* no fewer than fifty-two species of the *Lapponicum* series are listed. From the gardener's point of view there has been a great deal of splitting of hairs. Many are so closely allied as to be practically one and the same plant. In addition a number are of little garden importance. You may admire a hill-side covered with heather, but you would not care to grow any of the individual plants in your garden. It is the same with many of this series. We have tried to pick out a dozen or so. There are two yellow species, *R. chryseum* and *R. flavidum.*

The former is a small bush about 2 feet high, with small oval leaves about ½-inch long and very aromatic. The terminal truss has four to five flowers of a bright yellow in late April and May. *R. flavidum* is about the same height but rather more twiggy, and the pale-yellow flowers appear in late March. Personally we prefer *R. chryseum* not only because it is a brighter yellow, but because dwarfs that flower in March are much more likely to suffer from ground frost. But both are charming plants, and if you are sufficiently frost-free in early spring, certainly grow *R. flavidum* as well as *R. chryseum* (*R. chryseum*, coloured plate, facing page 82).

The only white member of the *Lapponicum* series is *R. microleucum*, a neat little plant about 1½ feet tall with pure white flowers in April. Both this and the yellow-flowered species are useful for growing with those with lavender flowers.

R. drumonium is one of the smallest of this dwarf series, and a very neat little plant with leaves only ¼-inch long and single flowers of a good mauve-purple. As it only grows 1 foot high and about as much or a little more in diameter, it is a useful plant for a small rock garden.

R. edgarianum grows taller, between 2 and 3 feet, again with tiny leaves just over ¼-inch long, but the single rose-purple flowers are larger and star-shaped. Apart from being a good plant it is the latest in the series to flower, and often does not come out in the north until June. It is fairly slow growing.

R. fastigiatum is an upright-growing dwarf, reaching up to three feet, with leaves densely scaly on both surfaces and light-purple flowers carried four to five in a truss. While it is quite a good plant in its own rights, it is often sold under the name of *R. impeditum*, a relative with a different habit.

R. hippophaeoides is one of the best of the series. It is up to three feet in height. It is not a very twiggy plant, and the branches are inclined to be leggy, which is not a drawback as they are well clothed with its greyish leaves about $1\frac{1}{4}$ inches long and $\frac{1}{4}$- to $\frac{1}{2}$-inch wide. The truss is larger and more compact, with six to eight flowers in April/May. The colour varies from rose to a soft lavender-mauve. In its good forms this is one of the best of all dwarfs, quick growing and free-flowering, but it is better to buy a form with a stated colour, as the roses are not so good as the lavenders. It will grow in almost any situation, even in semi-boggy ground.

There has been a great deal of misnaming over *R. impeditum*. The colour varies from rose-purple through a light blue-purple to a deep purple-blue, but in all cases the plant is a low rounded shrublet with very short branchlets, and dark-green leaves about $\frac{1}{2}$-inch long and $\frac{1}{4}$-inch broad. If it is not compact with very short branchlets, it is almost certainly *R. fastigiatum*. The true species is an enchanting rock-garden plant, but it is very slow growing. It will grow under ordinary rock-garden conditions, but likes a good proportion of peat in the soil, and it must have perfect drainage.

R. idoneum is a similar cushion-type of shrublet but a little higher, about $1\frac{1}{2}$ feet. There are two flowers in the terminal inflorescence, very short-stalked, deep purple-blue with a much lighter, almost white, throat. At the end of April this is a charming dwarf. The foliage is dark and shiny.

R. intricatum, as its name implies, is intricately branched with grey-green leaves about $\frac{1}{3}$-inch long that show up the several-flowered trusses, usually of a good lavender. Because of its twiggy growth it should be watched, and if necessary pruned to shape. It is a pleasant little shrub and the colour combination of leaves and flowers is good. It flowers early in May (coloured plate, facing page 82).

R. lysolepis is a plant that is rather neglected. It is upright-growing and reaches 2 feet. The leaves, ½- to ¾-inch long, are very shiny above. The truss is always three-flowered, and the flowers are about 1 inch in diameter of a reddish-violet. They appear towards the end of April. We like this plant for its neat appearance (coloured plate, facing page 82).

R. orthocladum grows taller, up to four feet, with very scaly and aromatic foliage and two to three-flowered trusses of mauve flowers.

R. rupicola is smaller again, a bare one to two feet, with a lovely colour combination of bronze-green leaves and deep plum-crimson flowers in April/May in a three- to five-terminal truss. This is like an improved form of *R. achroanthum* which is also sometimes listed. *R. rupicola* should certainly be included in a collection of dwarfs.

R. russatum is taller, reaching 4 feet, with leaves 1 inch long, deep green above and rusty brown below. The four- to five-flowered truss is deep purple to purple-blue in colour with a white throat. There is a slightly smaller form that used to be called *R. cantabile*. This and *R. scintillans* are certainly the best of the deep blue-purple-flowered dwarfs, but it should be grown where the sun can catch its flowers at an angle. It flowers at the end of April.

Last but by no means least comes *R. scintillans*. This is a twiggy shrub of two to three feet with small narrow leaves, slightly grey-brown. The truss is three-flowered and varies from a good lavender-blue to a deep blue-purple. The latter was awarded an F.C.C. This is probably the best coloured of the *Lapponicum* series, and is an easy and hardy plant. It flowers in the latter half of April or early May. It is an essential plant for any collection of dwarfs, but it is bluer than most and we prefer to keep it separated in a position by itself, or near one of the dwarfer hybrids like Blue Diamond.

Lepidotum series

This is another in the group of very lepidote rhododendrons that are centred in the series *Boothii*, *Glaucum*, *Lepidotum* and *Uniflorum*. While they differ in their scales on the foliage and in their styles, it is often difficult to separate them in cultivation. The *Lepidotum* series is again divided into two subseries, *Lepidotum* and *Baileyi*. *R. baileyi* is the sole member of its subseries. It is a spreading shrub up to 5 feet with leaves about 2 inches long, very scaly below with rust-coloured scales. The truss is terminal, with usually five to nine flowers, each about ¾-inch long, wide open, on long flower-stalks. The colour is reddish-purple or deep-purple. The lighter-coloured forms are attractive plants, free-flowering and fairly hardy. In addition they are useful, as they do not flower until May. *R. lepidotum*, in its own subseries, is a most variable plant, of which some forms from lower altitudes are not too hardy. It is a much smaller shrub with smaller leaves. One to three flowers are carried in a small truss again, with long flower-stalks. The colour varies from yellow to deep purple. Except that it flowers in June this plant is not exciting, although the yellow form is quite attractive.

A new species, *R. lowndesii*, has recently been described belonging to this subseries and is now in cultivation as seedlings. Nothing is known as yet of its behaviour in cultivation, but it sounds as if it might be an attractive plant. It grows in rock crevices at a great altitude, with pale dull-yellow flowers, spotted yellow ochre. The back of the corolla and the calyx is marked with carmine, and so are the flower-stems. The leaves are bright green and are apparently deciduous. It comes from Nepal at about 13,000 feet.

Maddenii series

This is a large series of mainly tender and often epiphytic shrubs, varying in size from dwarf to tall straggling plants. The flowers are usually funnel-shaped and waxy in texture, and often sweetly scented. From a gardening point of view many of the species are too close together to make their separate identification at all easy, and several are not in cultivation. At the moment the series is divided into three subseries : the *Maddenii* with fifteen or more stamens and ten to twelve ovary cells, *Megacalyx* with under twelve stamens and large calyx, and *Ciliicalyx* with small ciliate calyx and leaf-stalks with a V-shaped groove on the upper side.

Maddenii subseries

In cultivation *R. crassum* is a shrub up to ten or twelve feet high, heavily leafed with glossy and conspicuously veined leaves, and rusty scales below. The truss is three- to five-flowered with flowers about three inches long, narrowly funnel-shaped, densely scaly on the outside, pure white and scented. They are produced in June in the south and July in the north. This is probably one of the hardiest of the whole series, and we have grown it in Perthshire for many years. While the growth is never cut, the flower-buds are not absolutely winter-hardy. They will stand twelve or so degrees of frost, but not more. Thus it is not really a plant, for colder parts of the country, and it is too large for ordinary greenhouse cultivation.

R. maddenii is not so tall growing as *R. crassum* with narrower leaves. The truss has two to four flowers and they are shorter and wider than those of *R. crassum*. The colour is white with faint rose flush. This is a fairly tender plant, but is a suitable size for a large greenhouse, or can be grown outside in the extreme west and south-west. *R. manipurense* is larger, with one or two more flowers in the truss, and both leaves and flowers are larger. The colour is pure white. This is a very fine plant for very sheltered gardens in the west, and like *R. maddenii* it flowers in June.

R. polyandrum is a 3-foot bush, equally tender, with smaller oblong leaves 3 inches long and about 1 inch wide. The truss is five-flowered with flowers large for the size of the plant, and a large bunch of twenty-five stamens. The colour is white or pale yellow. This is an excellent plant for greenhouse cultivation.

Maddenii series : Megacalyx subseries

This undoubtedly possesses the largest-flowered and most sweetly scented plants in the series.

R. dalhousiae has been in cultivation for over a hundred years. While epiphytic in nature, in cultivation it is a thin straggling shrub with large tubular white flowers flushed with pink. It is definitely tender, but will grow outside in the extreme south-west ; a good greenhouse plant.

R. lindleyi is very similar with pure-white flowers and as deliciously scented. It is slightly hardier. *R. taggianum* again is similar, but usually with only three flowers to the truss compared to the others which have four to six flowers. The colour is pure white with a yellow blotch inside the base. It also is fragrant. This has proved definitely hardier than the other two in Cornwall and at Exbury, and also grows well on the west coast of Scotland. Elsewhere it makes a charming greenhouse plant.

These three species have been introduced several times, and it is difficult to make a choice between them. On the whole, typical *R. taggianum* is the best of the three, but we have seen *R. lindleyi* at Glenarn in Dunbartonshire, a form introduced by Ludlow and Sherriff, that is better than the average.

R. megacalyx is quite distinct. It is a large shrub with a five-flowered truss that smells of nutmeg. The flowers are almost prognathous as the lower lobes are longer than the upper. This is more tender and should be grown inside unless the garden is frost-free. It flowers in May or June, and is very lovely.

The largest flowers of all are to be found in *R. nuttallii* where the five- or six-flowered truss has flowers four or five inches long, a real trumpet and very sweetly scented. The colour varies, and may be creamy, pale yellow with or without green stripes down the outside, or almost white. All are good. This comes from such a low altitude in Bhutan that it is really satisfactory nowhere outside in the British Isles, but it makes a magnificent plant in a large greenhouse. *R. rhabdotum*, also from Bhutan, is not nearly so large with funnel-shaped flowers about three inches long, but quite distinct as its flowers are white with bright red lines down the back of the lobes. We have only seen it in flower once, a most striking plant. It is hardy in the extreme west and south-west and is successfully grown at Brodick in Arran.

Maddenii series : Ciliicalyx subseries

With the exception of *R. ciliatum* and *R. valentinianum* all the members of this subseries can only be grown outside in the mildest gardens in the south-west and west. We shall start with the two that are moderately hardy. *R. ciliatum* is a small shrub growing to 4 and 5 feet and widely spreading. The leaves are elliptic up to 3 inches long and $1\frac{1}{2}$ broad, hairy above and slightly scaly below. The two- to four-flowered truss has 2-inch long nodding flowers with a wide tube, white tinged with rose. As it flowers in April, it is often caught by spring frosts. In other respects it is quite hardy, but we find that in the north it is much better if it is grown in full sun. But beware of anything approaching a frost-pocket.

R. valentinianum is a pretty little plant $1\frac{1}{2}$ to 3 feet high with neat oval leaves $1\frac{1}{4}$ inches long, hairy on the margins and densely scaly below. There are two forms in cultivation, one introduced by Rock, taller-growing with larger and more pointed leaves and palish-yellow flowers ; the other with smaller rounder leaves margined with golden hairs and butter-yellow flowers. This does not grow more than $1\frac{1}{2}$ feet high. Both are good plants, but we prefer the smaller, which we have grown for many years in a situation in our glen that gets no wind. It is possibly in too much shade, but it flowers almost every year in late April, and is not often cut by spring frosts. Both forms are much hardier than has been supposed.

The other species in the *Ciliicalyx* subseries can be dealt with briefly as the flowers are all more or less widely funnel-shaped, and being epiphytes in nature are inclined to be straggly in cultivation. Except in the very mildest gardens in the west they should be grown in a greenhouse.

Maddenii series : Ciliicalyx subseries, R. johnstonianum
(*two-thirds natural size*)

R. *burmanicum* is a low compact shrub with yellow sweet-scented flowers. R. *ciliicalyx* is the best of the group with a small truss of lovely wide-open white or pale rose-coloured flowers. It flowers usually in April under glass. R. *formosum* is a close relation, but the leaves are fringed with long white hairs and the flowers are white tinged with yellow and with five rose-coloured stripes outside, sometimes very faint. It flowers later in May and June.

R. *johnstonianum* is a large spreading bush, again not unlike those mentioned above. The flowers are white spotted with red inside the back lobe and have a yellow blotch. But this is a variable plant in flower, and we have seen some mediocre forms. On the other hand it is hardier than most of them, and will grow outside in colder gardens, although it may not always flower satisfactorily. *R. taronense* is larger growing and also has white flowers with a yellow blotch, but it is verging on the more fleshy flowers that are associated with the *Megacalyx* subseries. Finally there is the semi-dwarf *R. veitchianum*, not much more than three feet, with a five-flowered truss with flowers quite large for the size of the plant, sometimes three inches long, white slightly tinged on the outside with green. It is a good greenhouse plant.

R. moupinense is placed in a series with two other species not in cultivation, but it is very close to the *Maddenii* series. It is a small shrub, but spreading like so many epiphytes are when planted in the ground, quite hardy but so early flowering, in February, that it is almost invariably frosted in cold districts. The leaves are about one inch long, ovate and rounded at both ends, very thick and leathery. The inflorescence is either one- or three-flowered, broadly funnel-shaped like in so many of the *Maddenii* series. The colour is white, or, more rarely, a charming pink ; and it is always sweetly scented. In cold districts it is an excellent plant for a cool greenhouse, and it makes a good pot-plant.

Neriiflorum series

This is a series of small to medium-sized shrubs, and for the ordinary gardener is one of the most important, as the plants are hardy and never get out of hand. Thus they are suitable for small gardens wherever they can be sheltered from the wind and given a certain amount of shade depending on the part of the country. Most of them flower in April or May ; thus they may suffer flower-damage from spring frosts, but the flower-buds of most of them will go through almost zero weather without harm. There are four subseries. While there are creeping plants at the one extreme and shrubs up to fifteen feet at the other, they all have a loose inflorescence. The corolla is unspotted and almost always waxy and fleshy in texture. The flowers are almost all tubular-campanulate.

Neriiflorum series : Forrestii subseries

There has been a great deal of confusion in the past in separating and naming the various forms of what used to be called *R. repens* and its varieties. On the one hand there is the creeping small round-leaved shrub, on the other the more upright growing shrub up to three feet with large rounded leaves that used to be called *R. repens* var. *chamae-thomsonii*. In between lay a number of forms running one into the other. What makes it more complicated for the gardener is that some plants from a single number may be very shy in flowering, while others from the same seed packet may be very free-flowering year after year. Thus it is of little value to state that Ward X or Forrest Y are particularly good plants. Luckily all forms can be propagated from cuttings fairly freely and from layers in the creeping forms, and so good flowering forms are coming into more general circulation.

At the moment they have been grouped under the following names and varieties :

R. forrestii was the name first given to a very creeping form in which the undersurface of the leaves was dull red. Those with a green undersurface were called *R. repens*. It is obvious that the green and red undersurface is not a correct diagnostic mark. As *R. forrestii* was the first to be named, the name remains, and the small-leaved glaucous-green under-surfaced form is called *R. forrestii* var. *repens*. As a general rule these very creeping forms are the shyest to flower. Unless a plant is known to come from a clone that is free-flowering it should be looked on with suspicion. The leaf-scales are noticeably persistent on the branches and give a shaggy effect. The leaves are obovate or round, up to one inch long. The flowers are almost always solitary, about one inch long, deep crimson with very definite nectar pouches at their base.

Then there is a form *R. forrestii* var. *tumescens*, that is more dome-shaped in the middle, while the outer branches creep, and which has larger leaves. In this there are one or two clones that flower freely and regularly. It also contains one number, Ward 6935, where the flowers are pink and reddish-purple instead of the usual bright scarlet, or crimson.

The taller plants have been called *R. chamae-thomsonii*. This is a plant with larger leaves, up to three inches long and one inch wide with a rounded apex. Instead of a one-to two-flowered inflorescence it usually has four to six, crimson-scarlet, rose-pink or occasionally white.

A little smaller in height and in foliage, and returning round the circle towards *R. forrestii* var. *tumescens*, is *R. chamae-thomsonii* var. *chamaethauma*. In this the colour is almost always deep crimson. Both of these taller forms have clones that flower freely.

All are equally hardy and flower in April/May. The dwarfer forms are better planted on a bank where they can begin to flow downhill, a natural form of growth. One point must be remembered in the cultivation of these and other plants in the series that form compact and tightly packed tops. Leaves and pine needles and other debris will work their way under the uppermost twigs and begin to rot. This in time will spread to the plant. We have seen several fine

plants of *R. forrestii* and *R. aperantum* with the centres completely rotted away. Under dry conditions they should be
shaken once or twice a year so that the debris falls to the base
of the plant where it can function as it was meant to do,
as a mulch. Well mulched, all this subseries will stand a fair
amount of sun. If they are in too much shade, even the best
clones will not flower so freely.

Neriiflorum series : Haematodes subseries

This subseries is quite distinct with its thick indumentum and
broad leaves rounded at the apex.

R. *beanianum* is a shrub of 4 to 5 feet with bristly
young branches. The leaves are 3 to 4 inches long and
1½ inches broad with typical rounded ends, very dark green
above and rough, with dark cinnamon-coloured indumentum below. The flowers are usually scarlet or dark red, but
may be pink. As it is April flowering, it is liable to be
damaged by spring frosts. It is an excellent plant in the
Home Counties, and we have admired it at Tower Court.
We have had it too short a time in Perthshire to make any
definite statement on its behaviour with us. It would seem,
however, to be on a par with *R. chaetomallum*, which is fairly
satisfactory if there are no April frosts.

One of the best plants in the whole series is *R. catacosmum*,
unfortunately rare. It is close to *R. haematodes* but taller, up
to 6 to 7 feet. The leaves are larger and more rounded,
up to 5 inches long and 2½ inches broad. The indumentum
is thick and pale cinnamon. The truss is rather more lax
than usual, with about nine very fleshy wider-open flowers,
rose-crimson with conspicuous pouches at the base. Most
distinct of all is the large calyx, which actually forms a secondary cup almost 1 inch long, and is often tinted with rose.

R. chaetomallum is not quite typical of the subseries, as it has thinner branchlets and sometimes the indumentum is not nearly so woolly. We have several forms, varying from those with the usual thick cinnamon-coloured indumentum that persists to one that loses it in the mature leaf. This is a smaller shrub than *R. catacosmum*, not exceeding 5 feet. The leaves are about 3½ inches long and 1¾ inches broad. The truss has four to six tubular-campanulate flowers, not quite so fleshy as those in *R. catacosmum*, almost 2 inches long. The usual colour is scarlet to deep crimson, very pure and with no blue.

Although it flowers in April, on the whole *R. chaetomallum* is a satisfactory plant, but it does not like drought. We have never seen a form of a poor colour.

The best garden plant in the subseries is undoubtedly *R. haematodes*. In nature it apparently reaches 10 feet, but in gardens it seems to remain as a widely spreading, more or less flat-topped bush of about 3 feet tall, and as much as 6 feet in diameter. The leaves are 3 to 4 inches long and 1½ inches wide, usually round at the apex with a definite mucro, dark green and glabrous above with the veins clearly seen, and a very thick woolly persisting indumentum below. The truss has six to eight flowers, very fleshy and tubular-campanulate, 2 inches long with 1-inch pedicels. The colour is almost always a rich crimson or crimson-scarlet.

One great advantage of *R. haematodes* is that it flowers in May. We also find that the flowers do not all appear at the same time. Thus if we are unfortunate enough to have a May frost, by no means all the flowers are damaged. While this belongs to a class of rhododendron that forms table-top thickets, it is so shapely in form that we prefer seeing it by itself and not crowded by other plants. It tends to grow faster outwards than upright.

R. mallotum is much taller in growth, tending to form a few stout upright branches or to be actually tree-like. The leaves are the thickest and the largest in the series, often 2 inches longer than those of *R. haematodes*, very dark green and rough on the surface, and the richest cinnamon-red indumentum that feels like felt. It is almost the same coloured indumentum as that in *R. bureavii*. The truss is compact and carries about fourteen flowers, dark crimson in colour.

This is too early-flowering, early March, for colder parts of the country. Apart from that we have grown several plants on different occasions, and it does not like our conditions. It is, however, such a handsome plant that no frost-free garden in the west or south should be without it. In order to show off its indumentum it should be viewed if possible from below.

Another early flowering species for western gardens is *R. pocophorum*, fairly close to *R. catacosmum*, but with smaller calyces to the flowers. It carries a heavy truss of about twelve to fifteen flowers, equally fleshy, crimson and sometimes faintly spotted.

Neriiflorum series : Neriiflorum subseries

In this subseries there are one or two plants like *R. neriiflorum* itself which have no indumentum. The leaves are evenly oblong-elliptic, tapering equally at both ends. Others have also narrower leaves than in the other subseries, but they have an indumentum that is usually not persisting. The foliage-buds are sharply pointed.

R. floccigerum is a shrub up to 5 feet, with narrow leaves up to 5 inches long and barely 1 inch wide, with a loose reddish indumentum that soon disappears and leaves the undersurface almost white. The truss has four to seven flowers, about $1\frac{1}{2}$ inches long, with nectar pouches at the base. They are fleshy and pink to crimson in colour. This flowers in March in the south, in April with us. We like it, as a useful plant that causes very little trouble and seems to grow in almost any situation without fussing. But care should be taken to choose one of the better forms, as there are also dirty yellow forms which should be avoided.

R. neriiflorum reaches 5 or 6 feet, or up to 15 feet in its taller form, often listed under the name *R. euchaites*. *R. neriiflorum* is spreading with thinner branches, and no indumentum on its foliage. The leaves vary from $2\frac{1}{2}$ to 5 inches long and 1 to 2 inches wide. The inflorescence is just as variable and may contain from five to twelve flowers about $1\frac{1}{2}$ inches long, and has the usual tubular-campanulate shape of the series, always of a bright scarlet-crimson. It flowers in April/May (coloured plate, facing page 18).

This is an essential plant for every sheltered garden. While it is variable in size, and indeed in hardiness, for some forms are more tender than others, yet it is essentially a fine garden plant, flowering every year, and starting to flower at a fairly small size. It should be grown in half-shade, and must be sheltered from cold winds. There is a form that does not start to grow until late July which should be avoided.

R. sperabile is not unlike *R. neriiflorum,* but it has an indumentum, whitish in colour, that usually persists, and the truss only carries four to five flowers. It is not so important, nor so hardy.

Neriiflorum series : Sanguineum subseries

This consists of a number of small shrubs, most of which are still in a state of flux ; thus they are not fixed species. Some are undoubtedly natural hybrids.

At one time no fewer than thirty-nine different species were named in this one subseries. Now they have been reduced to eight species and a number of subspecies ; and some of these subdivisions have no horticultural importance. The differences are almost entirely those of flower colour and whether there are glands or not on the ovary. To show how puzzled the botanists have been, it is only necessary to point out, that of the original thirty-nine named species no less than fourteen were collected on one mountain mass, Kenyichumpo in the upper reaches of the Salween river. It is almost impossible that these could all be fixed species in one subseries. There must be a number of natural hybrids among them.

R. aperantum is the dwarfest of the subseries, a plant rarely exceeding $1\frac{1}{2}$ feet in height but often 3 feet in diameter. The two definite diagnostic marks are the persistent bud-scales in the young shoots and the margins of the leaves which are almost always recurved. The truss is four-flowered on pedicels almost 1 inch long. The flowers as usual are tubular-campanulate about 2 inches long. The colour is exceedingly varied, white, yellow, orange, pink or scarlet, or combinations of any of them.

This is a typical table-top plant of the high moors in and near Upper Burma. So close are the plants wedged together that it is sometimes possible to walk on the top of them without your feet going through to the ground beneath. In cultivation it grows well enough and is quite hardy, but it is not an easy plant to flower with any freedom ; nor can we make any suggestions, unless that it might be grown with more success in almost full sun and exposure. It is a pity that it is not proving free-flowering in cultivation, as mats of it in full flower are extremely lovely.

R. citriniflorum is slightly taller, and is almost half-way between *R. chaetomallum* of the *Haematodes* subseries and a typical member of the *Sanguineum* subseries, as the under-surface of the leaves have a spongy fawn-coloured indumentum. The truss consists of four to six flowers, usually bright lemon-yellow, occasionally rose or crimson but always with a yellow undertone.

We have found this even more difficult. In the course of years we have lost a number of plants. Like *R. aperantum* it flowers in April. Nor have we seen really good plants in any other collection.

R. dichroanthum is a larger, more spreading shrub, sometimes reaching 6 feet. The leaves are more spoon-shaped with a wide and rounded apex, and an indumentum that is sometimes thin and sometimes woolly, greyish-white or fawn. It flowers late in May in the south, usually in June in the north. It has a large cup-shaped calyx, and the colour varies from bronze, through mustard (which should be avoided), to a good orange and orange-pink.

This is a useful late-flowering species, and much easier to grow in half-shade ; but it is imperative that good forms are grown, as some of the mustard colours are hideous. Older collections may have them growing under the names of subspecies such as *R. apodectum, R. herpesticum* and *R. scypho-calyx*. As a rule the first named produced the best forms.

R. parmulatum is a plant of which we have had no personal experience, but it has proved attractive and hardy in the

Royal Botanic Garden in Edinburgh. It is a typical member of the *sanguineum* alliance, with a cup-shaped calyx, but the colour is unique in the series, creamy white with dark plum-coloured markings and the same colour staining the basal pouches.

R. sanguineum shows so many variations that it obviously forms an alliance of plants in the process of forming species and of natural hybrids. As a rule they form plants about four to five feet high with stiff branches and leathery oval leaves, the under-surface often with a greyish-white skin. The inflorescence consists of three to four flowers with narrow tubular-campanulate corollas.

The original plant had flowers of dark crimson with its subspecies *haemaleum* so dark as to be black-crimson, only attractive with a low sun behind the flowers, and so of little value in the garden. The same applies to subspecies *didymum*. The best forms are to be seen in the subspecies *roseotinctum*, which varies from creamy white margined with rose through soft rose to an attractive yellow tipped with rose. As a rule plants of the *sanguineum* alliance grow and flower as well in colder gardens as in the south. They keep more in character in the north and east than in the milder west. They are not very shapely plants by themselves, and are better planted in groups of three or four fairly close together.

Ponticum series

Owing to the prevalence of *R. ponticum* as a woodland weed in many parts of the country, the whole series for years was considered to be of little garden value. This, of course, was a great mistake. Apart from the fact that many of them will bear comparison in general comeliness with other series from China they are almost all of cast-iron hardiness, although some are definitely slow-growing. The series is divided into geographical subseries *Caucasicum*, including the Caucasus, North Asia ; Formosa and Japan, and *Ponticum*, including North America, Europe and Asia Minor. Within the series there are great variations. The distinguishing features which remain throughout for the most part are the elongation of the flower axis, which produces what is called candelabroid growth, and the funnel-campanulate corolla which is deeply cut into oblong lobes. In this they are like those in some of the lepidote series such as the *Triflorum* series, Thus the lobes are almost exactly the same length as the tube.

Ponticum series : Caucasicum subseries

R. adenopodum is an exception as it is almost the only member of the series that comes from China. It will form a bush 8 to 10 feet high with long narrow leaves, almost 10 inches long by $2\frac{1}{2}$ inches wide, smooth and dark green above. Six to eight flowers are carried in a loose corymb with a noticeably long rachis. The 2-inch flowers are pale rose, unspotted in the best forms.

A useful hardy but not very exciting plant.

The same might be said about *R. brachycarpum*, a many-branched shrub of about six feet. The leaves are somewhat similar to those of *R. catawbiense* with a thin white indumentum. The truss is large, up to twenty, one-inch flowers, creamy white with indeterminate green spots. It flowers in July.

R. caucasicum itself is still something of a mystery. The original description was of a plant rarely more than 3 feet in height with obovate leaves, dark green above and a thin tawny tomentum on the undersurface. The truss is elongated with many $1\frac{1}{2}$-inch flowers, yellowish or pale rose. The odd thing is that the original description did not mention yellow flowers, and yet the old variety called Cunningham's Sulphur would appear to be nearest the description of true *R. caucasicum* apart from the flower colour.

In old gardens there are still varieties called *caucasicum album* and *caucasicum pictum*, which must have a high percentage of *caucasicum* blood, although the shape of the corolla is not the same as that of Cunningham's Sulphur. In addition, the early flowering Christmas Cheer is possibly very near to true *R. caucasicum*, although to a certain extent it lacks the elongated truss.

In any case both Cunningham's Sulphur and Christmas Cheer are very useful plants in cold gardens. The latter never comes into flower all at once, and if the first or second, or even third, trusses are frosted, there are more to follow on. In a mild winter it will start to flower in December.

Another plant that has long been a name in our older gardens is *R. metternichii*. The true species has a seven-lobed corolla, whereas almost all the plants in cultivation are five-lobed. This means that the name must be changed to *R. degronianum*. This forms a compact bush of three to four feet, often broader than it is high, and particularly well clothed right to the base. The long and narrowish leaves are dark glossy green above, and thickly felted below with a tawny or reddish indumentum. The elongated truss has twelve flowers, about two inches long, a soft pink with deeper pink lines running down the outside of the petals. It flowers in May.

This is a good plant where a ground cover of medium height is required. It is quite hardy and will stand a good deal of sun.

R. hyperythrum in its best forms is one of the finest plants

Ponticum series : Caucasicum subseries, R. degronianum
(*two-thirds natural size*)

in the series. It is a small bush, usually wider than it is tall, with narrowly oblong leathery leaves, up to 5 inches long and $1\frac{1}{2}$ inches wide, and no indumentum. The usual elongated truss has about twelve flowers, five-lobed in March. In the best forms these are a pure snow-white. In others they are spotted with purple.

As this fine plant comes from Formosa, it is not so hardy as the rest of the series ; and it is early flowering. There is a lovely form of it at Tower Court.

R. makinoi is not unlike a narrow-leaved *R. degronianum*, but the bush is a little more rounded, the leaves are much narrower and the flowers appear in June. We have no personal experience of this plant. It should be useful in cold gardens owing to its late flowering and later growth, while its very narrow leaves are unusual.

R. smirnowii is a wide-spreading shrub of about six feet with leaves about the same size as *R. ponticum*, but more leathery with a thick pale-brown felt. In the young foliage this is an attractive white. The flowers are like those of *R. ponticum*, and also appear in June.

This is a very hardy plant, in many ways more attractive than *R. ponticum*, particularly in its young growth. It is deservedly popular as a hardy rhododendron in the colder districts of the United States. It has a very close relative in *R. ungernii* with larger leaves and more flowers in the truss.

R. yakusimanum is a comparative newcomer from Japan. It is 3 feet high and broader than it is tall, very compact in growth. The young growth and foliage have a greyish-white tomentum which disappears on the upper surface and turns brown below. The truss is not so elongated as in most of the series, and carries about twelve bell-shaped flowers, pink in the bud and opening almost pure white. This attractive plant deservedly won a First Class Certificate in 1947. It flowers in May, is very free flowering and is worthy of more general cultivation.

Ponticum series : Ponticum subseries

In this the texture of the leaves is softer and there is no indumentum on the mature foliage.

R. californicum is the western counterpart of *R. catawbiense*. It is a shrub of six to twelve feet. The tall truss carries twenty or more flowers, white or pink or rose, marked with yellowish spots. While attractive in its native state in big drifts of varying tones and shades, it is hardly good enough when grown as a single plant for gardens in the British Isles.

R. catawbiense is the American equivalent of *R. ponticum*. It has been largely used as a parent for cast-iron hybrids both in the United States and, in the nineteenth century, in this country. If left to itself it will go on layering itself until it forms a huge thicket. There is one at Balbirnie in Fife that must be nearly fifty feet in diameter.

R. maximum is looser in habit, larger in foliage and with a larger calyx. The colour varies from white through light rose to purplish-magenta, with yellow-green spots on the upper lobe. It is also of cast-iron constitution.

R. ponticum is so well known that it can be passed over.

Saluenense series

This is a very distinct series of dwarf plants, often prostrate. The distinguishing character is the shape of the corolla which is wide open with a very short tube, usually scaly on the outside.

R. calostrotum will grow to 2 feet with stiff branchlets. The leaves are about 1 inch long by ½ inch broad with greyish scales. The inflorescence is two- to three-flowered on long flower stalks, bright rose-magenta or magenta-purple or occasionally crushed strawberry pink, produced in May in the south, June in the north. The variety *calciphilum* has smaller leaves, but otherwise is very similar.

This is a useful rock-garden plant. It is a pity that this along with the rest of the series tends to magenta in the colour of its flowers, as they are large and showy for the size of the plants. It is better if they are kept by themselves, and in any case kept away from lavenders or blues.

R. chameunum is usually not more than one foot high, very bushy and compact. The leaves are smaller, very dark green that usually turns to a dull reddish-green in winter. The

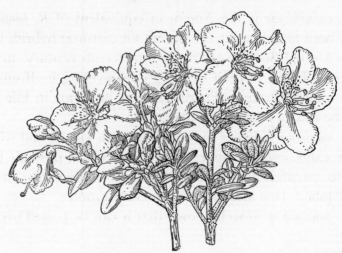

Saluenense series : R. calostrotum
(*two-thirds natural size*)

flowers are a deep rose-purple with crimson markings. It is June flowering and sometimes bears a second crop of flowers in the autumn. While quite hardy, it dislikes dry conditions during the growing season, and should not be grown in full sun unless in a damp situation.

Closely allied to the last is *R. keleticum*, but it is semi-prostrate in habit, forming a low mound. It is this habit which is its great attraction, dark green and glossy and very closely branched. The flowers, also appearing in June, are too dark a magenta-purple to be showy.

R. nitens forms a small erect shrub, up to two feet in height. The flowers are much lighter than in most of the series. We have seen forms almost pinkish-rose, and most attractive plants. It is a good garden plant, although slow-growing, as it flowers in the end of June or July, and this prolongs the season.

R. prostratum on the other hand flowers in April, and is not a particularly easy plant in many gardens. It forms a

low shrublet, 4 inches high. The colour of the flowers is a
curious shade of deep pink with a violet background.

R. *radicans* is a much better garden plant, but like R. *prostratum* it must have moisture in the growing season and
should not be grown in full sun. The form introduced by
Rock, that more commonly seen, forms a low mound with
the outer branchlets hugging the ground. The older introduction by Forrest, a rarer and not quite such an easily grown
plant, is completely prostrate. Rock's form is close to R.
keleticum. In both cases the growth is closely matted. The
flowers are borne singly in late May or June well above the
growth and show up well against the dark-green narrow
polished leaves. The colour is purple. This is an excellent
plant once it is established, and once it feels at home it
spreads quite rapidly and flowers freely.

The type species, R. *saluenense*, is the tallest growing in
the series, and if grown in half-shade in good soil will make
a bush 4 feet each way. Its worst fault is that when mature
the main branches are very easily broken by snow. We had
one plant where every branch was split at a branch-fork by
a heavy fall. The leaves are even larger than those of
R. *calostrotum*, and are often an attractive grey-green colour
that shows off the purple-crimson flowers with darker markings that appear early in May.

This is an excellent garden plant, but it should be planted
in rather less shade than many of them to prevent it from
becoming too leggy.

Scabrifolium series

This series is very close to the *Virgatum* series, differing chiefly
in the fact that it is much more pubescent. They are all
small shrubs, most of them 3 to 4 feet high, with long

shoots and narrow lanceolate leaves, about 1 to 1½ inches long. The flowers are all axillary, and are clustered towards the top of the branches. While most of them are pretty plants, and almost all are given three stars, they flower in April or earlier, and so are not exactly plants for cold gardens. We have grown a number of them from time to time, but in almost all cases they have been badly cut in three years out of four. The growth follows very rapidly after flowering, and this is also liable to be damaged. On the other hand we have seen lovely plants of *R. scabrifolium* at Exbury, and have particularly admired the rarer *R. spiciferum* at Brodick on the island of Arran, while *R. spinuliferum* is a common and lovely plant in Cornwall.

R. hemitrichotum is a small shrub of 3 feet. The small flowers, about ¾-inch long, are produced up the stem rather more than at the apex, and are brick-red in the bud, changing to soft pink or white as they open in April. We have not found it an easy shrub to flower, and this applies, we think, to other gardens as well.

R. mollicomum is taller, growing up to five feet with long whippy branches. The flowers are crimson in the best forms or rose, also quite pretty. What we said about *R. hemitrichotum* applies equally to *R. mollicomum*.

R. pubescens is like a hairy and rather leggy *R. racemosum*, with pink flowers. We would rather grow the latter under all circumstances.

R. scabrifolium has equally long and whippy branches. The pink and white flowers come out in March. Oddly enough, although this looks a softer plant, and is, of course, often cut by frost, yet it is actually better able to withstand our springs than some of its relatives. We grow both the pink and the white forms, and prefer the latter.

Scabrifolium series : R. scabrifolium
(*two-thirds natural size*)

R. spiciferum is a rare plant of which we have had no practical experience. It flowers in April and, while spreading, is not so straggling. Its shoots are covered with rich pink flowers. It certainly is lovely, as good as, if not better, than the best form of *R. racemosum*. We have seen a number of plants and the colour does not seem to vary. If we lived in the west we would certainly not be without it.

R. spinuliferum grows up to 6 or more feet with larger foliage, 2 to 3 inches long and $1\frac{1}{2}$ inches broad, rough on the upper surface. This species has peculiar upright flowers unlike most other rhododendrons. They form a tube, rather pinched at each end, and with protruding stamens. The colour is crimson or brick-red. April-flowering.

This is definitely a tender plant, only fit for southern or western gardens. You either like it or you don't. We are not wildly enthusiastic and look upon it more as a curiosity, although some enthusiasts praise it highly. Possibly we are too orthodox.

Stamineum series

This is a series that grows under more or less tropical conditions, so none of them are suitable for growing outside in the British Isles. Most of them are small trees, and the inflorescence is axillary. In almost all the flowers are narrowly funnel-shaped, five-lobed, with strikingly exerted stamens. Botanically they are nearest to the *Ovatum* series. Very few are in cultivation, but one, *R. stenaulum*, which lives in Upper Burma and adjacent lands, is occasionally introduced. We have never heard of its coming to a successful maturity outside in Britain. The flowers are fragrant and a purplish-rose.

Taliense series

This is a large series of dwarf to medium shrubs, the foliage of most of which has a thick indumentum. This is by no means a popular series. Many are dull plants and they are often very slow in coming to a flowering stage, but rhododendron enthusiasts anxious for quick returns are apt to condemn the entire series. There are some, however, that are quite attractive, and one or two are charming garden plants, whose only fault is the time they take to flower. One thing in their favour is that they are all very hardy, and once they have come to flowering size most of them flower freely whatever the season may be.

One of the reasons for their unpopularity is undoubtedly

the fact that because many of them are widespread in nature, collectors sent home the same plant far too often under different numbers. These were grown in quantity in the early days of rhododendron enthusiasm, only to be thrown out as a complete waste of time. Members of the series were collected under eighty-nine different numbers in Forrest's 1917–19 expedition alone.

With the exception of the *Roxieanum* subseries, which is conspicuous for its tight little trusses and narrow incurved leaves, the others are separated by botanical characteristics not easily noticed by the naked eye and of little horticultural distinction. While many are in cultivation, it is unlikely that the majority of them are now being propagated. The few that are worth growing are mentioned in alphabetical order, whatever their subseries may be.

R. adenogynum is a spreading shrub up to 6 feet, sometimes more, with stout branches. The leaves are long and narrow running to an acute point, up to 5 inches long and 1½ inches wide, dark green and glabrous above, with a thick tawny indumentum below. The terminal truss carries twelve flowers, which are funnel-campanulate and thick in texture, about 2 inches long, five-lobed. The colour is near white, rose or rose magenta with crimson markings. April-flowering.

This grows rather faster than many in the series and is quite attractive with its large trusses. Its habit is not unlike that of *R. insigne*. *R. adenophorum* is so close that it can be regarded as a synonym.

R. balfourianum is more upright and stiffer in growth, but does not exceed six to eight feet. The leaves are a little shorter and a little broader and the indumentum is not so felted. In its better forms the colour of the flowers is a rose-pink with crimson spots. This again is quite a good

Taliense series : R. adenogynum
(*two-thirds natural size*)

plant for an odd spot in the woodland. We find it does
not object to dry conditions. It is April-flowering in the
north.

R. bureavii forms a compact bush up to six feet. It is shy
to flower, but this is unimportant as it is a lovely foliage
plant. The upper surface of the leaves is dark green, while
below there is a thick bright rusty-red felt, a striking combination of foliage colour. It should be planted above the path
on a bank where the undersurface can be appreciated.

R. clementinae, a compact shrub with stiff branches. This
again is a most striking foliaged shrub in its best forms. The
leaves are wide oval, incurved, about six inches long by three
inches wide. The upper surface is dark mat green with a

bluish sheen, and the undersurface has a very pale fawn indumentum. When the leaf first unfolds, the indumentum is pale cream and the upper surface is a steely blue. Our plant certainly has the most beautiful rhododendron foliage that we have seen, but we have been told that this is a particularly good form. *R. clementinae* is slow-growing and slow to flower. It carries a large truss of about fifteen flowers more bell-shaped than in most of the series, creamy white to a bright rose with deeper crimson markings.

It has the reputation of being a somewhat difficult plant, but our specimen is growing in rather more than half-shade and is completely sheltered from the wind. It flowers in early May.

R. detonsum is taller growing, with equally stiff branches. It has the narrower leaves of *R. adenogynum*, with a loose indumentum that soon disappears leaving the undersurface cinnamon-coloured but smooth. The truss of ten flowers is very loose owing to the 2-inch pedicels. The flowers are larger, $2\frac{1}{2}$ inches long, a good rose-pink with a few crimson spots. This is the best in flower of the larger members of the series, and is worth growing in almost any collection.

R. gymnocarpum is one of the very slow-growing species in the *Roxieanum* subseries, never exceeding 3 feet in height, with thick leathery leaves 3 inches long by 1 inch to $1\frac{1}{2}$ inches wide and a semi-persistent fawn indumentum. The truss has three to four flowers, a deep crimson with even deeper markings.

This is the only member of the series with anything approaching red flowers and is worth growing where space is a consideration. It is April-flowering. From its appearance it might belong to the *Sanguineum* subseries of the *Neriiflorum* series.

In this *Roxieanum* subseries there are a number of forms so different in their extreme state that they must be given specific rank, but with intermediate forms joining them together. The general features are very short annual growths. They are very slow-growing, usually with narrow leaves coming to an acute point at the apex, with very marked incurving of the leaves, and a very tight truss of small flowers all heavily spotted.

The largest of these types, a plant that may reach 6 feet and is very bushy is called *R. russotinctum*. The plant with the narrowest leaves, sometimes only ¼ inch wide and very recurved is called *R. roxieanum* var. *oreonastes*, and the creeping form, a very rare but desirable plant of which we have had no experience, is called *R. pronum*. Mr R. B. Cooke has a fine plant of the last at Corbridge-on-Tyne.

Of these *R. roxieanum* and its variety *oreonastes* make charming garden plants, not only for the tufts of narrow dark-green leaves which sometimes hang for three or more years, but also for the delightful little round trusses, usually of pure-white flowers with numerous little crimson spots. These trusses may have fifteen or more flowers and yet be little bigger than a golf ball. Though very slow-growing, once they start to flower they rarely miss a year. We have a small group of them, rather ungainly and out of character by being overshaded during the war, but they are always much admired when in flower. Invariably the question is asked, What are they? They flower with us in late April.

Finally there are two plants collected by E. H. Wilson which are certainly good but are slow growing and rare in gardens. They are *R. wasonii*, a small bush of two to three feet with a loose truss of creamy-white flowers with crimson spots, and its pink form called *rhododactylum* with clear-pink flowers also spotted. These are useful plants owing to their neat habit and small size. In addition they flower at a comparatively early age.

Thomsonii series

This is one of the most important series from the garden point of view. It is divided into four subseries with a few anomalous plants between that might go in one or in another. One of the subseries, the *Selense*, is so slow to flower that with the possible exception of two species it can be ignored in cultivation.

The diagnostic marks in the entire series are difficult to define. As soon as you lay down any particular point, it must be qualified with a list of exceptions. And yet anyone who has worked for several years among rhododendrons knows instinctively in most cases when a plant comes within the orbit of the series. With the exception of *R. williamsianum*, all are shrubs of medium size. The foliage has no indumentum, and is smooth and mostly rather leathery to the feel. The leaves may be almost round, or oval or elliptic, but in all cases, whatever the shape, they are rounded at both ends and do not run to an acute point. The inflorescence is few flowered. In the *Thomsonii* and *Campylocarpum* subseries the corolla is campanulate, in the *Selense* subseries funnel-shaped and in the *Souliei* subseries saucer-shaped.

Thomsonii series : Campylocarpum subseries

R. callimorphum, now including *R. cyclium*, is rather an angular-branched shrub up to seven to eight feet in height and about five feet in diameter when mature. The leaves vary in shape and size but are often orbicular or oval. The loose truss is five- to eight-flowered with campanulate flowers, in some

127

forms more widely open than in others, pink to deep rose with or without a crimson blotch.

It is as variable in times of flowering as in other respects, but in all cases it is a plant for open woodland, and will not stand drought conditions or scorching. We find it an excellent plant in eastern Perthshire, where even the earlier forms do not come out until May, and our largest and best plant until June; but in the south we have seen some forms in full flower before the end of April. While they vary, all are pretty and graceful in flower and out. We have what is almost a microform with leaves the size of a shilling and small flowers of a good pink. It does not exceed four feet.

R. caloxanthum is rather smaller in height but similar in foliage. There are forms that are very like the well-known *R. campylocarpum*. In flower *R. caloxanthum* is very distinct. The buds are apricot or orange and open to a sulphur-yellow or pale orange, both charming and equally free-flowering. But it is not such a useful plant for cold districts as it flowers in April. The buds tend to show colour a considerable time before the flowers are fully out, and the moment there is a tint in them we find them inclined to be frost tender. In a frost-free spring they are among the most lovely of the smaller rhododendrons. *R. telopeum* with smaller leaves and flowers is so near *R. caloxanthum* that it can be counted as the same species.

R. campylocarpum is probably the best-known yellow-flowered rhododendron and one of the earliest to be introduced into this country from the Sikkim-Himalayas. There are two forms which are quite distinct, Hooker's original introduction, bushy and about six feet in height, with bright yellow flowers, and a taller form, var. *elatum*, from a lower elevation, apricot in the bud like *R. caloxanthum*, opening to paler yellow flowers. The former is the hardier form. Though both are quite hardy, they are actually better plants for the south and west. In colder districts their place should be taken by *R. wardii.*

Thomsonii series ; Selense subseries

This subseries differs in the shape of the leaves which are oblong, and in the shape of the corolla which is funnel-shaped. As mentioned above, its garden value is negligible owing to the length of time taken to flower freely, in many cases two decades or more. With large-leaved rhododendrons even the foliage is worth looking at, and the waiting-time is at least interesting, but as plants the *Selense* subseries lack character, although they are charming when in full flower. Thus we only mention two.

The first is *R. martinianum*, which proves the exception as it flowers at an earlier age than most of the subseries. It is a neat little plant up to four feet high with elliptic leaves up to two inches long and under one inch wide. The small truss has one to three flowers with long pedicels. The colour is pale rose or creamy white. It is April-flowering.

The second is *R. selense* itself, which is like a larger form of the last with more flowers to the truss. The colour is usually pink or rose, unspotted but with a small blotch. There are various subspecies with flowers of different colours. But they all take many years to flower.

Thomsonii series : Souliei subseries

This contains some of the best garden plants among all the species of rhododendron. According to the latest classification of the series it contains four species, two with yellow flowers, *R. wardii* and *R. litiense*, and two with white and pink, *R. puralbum* and *R. souliei.*

R. wardii in turn is a compound species, consisting at one time of seven so-called species. Thus it is obviously a very variable plant, ranging from 4 feet up to 12 feet in height with leaves either almost orbicular or oval or oblong, always with a rounded apex. The inflorescence is also variable, and may contain from five to twelve flowers all with a more or less long pedicel. The colour is always yellow, sometimes pale, sometimes deeper, sometimes with a crimson blotch, sometimes flowering early in May, sometimes in June (coloured plate, facing p. 66). All flowers are saucer-shaped, but we have one plant where they are as small as a sixpence, and another where they are over $2\frac{1}{2}$ inches wide. Thus it is difficult to differentiate between one form and another except to say that they are all good, and particularly useful in a cold garden in the later-flowering forms. If there are any which can be called more or less distinct from the typical orbicular-leaved species, it is that which used to be called *R. croceum*, where the foliage is thicker in texture and more oval in shape, while the flowers are a brighter yellow with no blotch. With us it flowers in June. There is also a Ludlow and Sherriff form with a blotch which is very good indeed.

The other which is still given specific rank is *R. litiense*. As they have removed *R. croceum*, we cannot quite follow why they have left *R. litiense*, as the only noticeable difference is that the leaves are more oblong, and the flowers are sometimes not quite so openly saucer-shaped, and are sometimes smaller. Where we do think they differ is that *R. wardii* and its alliance is more free-flowering on the whole than *R. litiense*, but that may be due to some local condition. In any case they are all plants of thin woodland. The soil need not be particularly peaty, but they do not like dry conditions.

R. *puralbum* and R. *souliei* in turn might be called colour forms of one and the same plant, because they are identical except in the colour of their flowers. They will both reach about nine feet in height, usually with ovate leaves very rounded at the base, but here again they vary in shape and size. The loose truss consists of five to eight flowers, the same shape as in R. *wardii*, pure white in R. *puralbum* and a pale pink in R. *souliei*. Again they tend to run into each other. We have a set of plants that are bright pink in the bud and pure white in the open flowers with no sign of pink. Are they R. *souliei* or R. *puralbum*?

Both are among the few rhododendrons that actually prefer the colder conditions of the east coast to the warm and damp of the west. Like R. *wardii* they are plants of thin woodland. With the bluish tinge in their leaves and their lovely flowers they are certainly among the finest of all rhododendron species. Flowering in late May, the flowers and the foliage are very rarely if ever damaged by spring frosts. R. *puralbum* in its original description is a very rare plant.

Thomsonii series : *Thomsonii subseries*

This subseries is closest related to the *Campylocarpum* subseries. Apart from a botanical difference of the absence of glands on the style, they are larger plants, many of them have prominent cup-shaped calyces, and on the whole the predominant colour of the flowers is crimson.

In their garden behaviour they are more plants for the south and west. Except for one rare plant R. *hylaeum*, which is May flowering, they all flower in April or earlier. Sometimes the plants themselves are hardy, but the flowers are so often cut as to make their cultivation in cold gardens rather unprofitable.

R. cyanocarpum is closely related to *R. thomsonii*, growing to the same height, about eighteen feet, and with the same blue-green, glabrous foliage, but the colour is never crimson, but creamy-white flushed rose, or soft rose, and occasionally pure white. The last is the most attractive. We have seen it in the south where it is one of the best white-flowered rhododendrons that we know. At Exbury they do not like the coloured forms, but the cream, stained with rose, is uncommon and attractive if there is no crimson or scarlet near it. Flowering in early April, it should be grown in frost-free gardens.

R. eclecteum is such a variable plant both in size and shape of leaf and in colour that it is not properly ' fixed ' as a species. The colour varies from white, yellow, pink or rose, spotted or unspotted. It is, however, a smaller plant and does not exceed seven feet in height. It may flower in January, February or March ; and is obviously not for cold gardens. We have not attempted to grow it, but we have seen in Cornwall a mixed vase of the various colours of *R. eclecteum*, and they are certainly attractive, as also is the young foliage.

Very close but with a longer petiole and a thin layer of hairs on the undersurface is *R. stewartianum*. The range of colour is even wider, as there are even crimson forms known. It also flowers in March and April. We have grown one or two plants for years, but cannot say that it flowers freely or that it escapes being cut by frost in most years.

R. hookeri is an old Himalayan introduction and a very fine plant. It will reach eighteen feet but is slow-growing. The oval leaves have isolated hair tufts on the lateral veins that to the touch feel almost like hooks. It has a large truss of deep-crimson funnel-shaped flowers that appear in March and April. Rothschild has noted that the growth starts very early and is almost always frosted. That may be so in the south. We had a plant for a number of years, that was ultimately flattened by a large walnut-tree falling on it during a gale. While it flowered in April it did not start into such precocious growth, and was rarely cut. But we have not replaced it, as we found the flower-buds were not at all frost hardy and were blackened by more than twelve degrees of frost. It is certainly one of the finest of the deep-crimson flowers, and should be far more often seen in the west.

R. meddianum, on the other hand, which is the Chinese equivalent of *R. thomsonii*, with us comes into growth far too early in the year. This is almost always cut. While it may send out second shoots, these are never vigorous and never ripen enough to produce a flower-bud. Apart from the fact that the leaves are more oblong-oval than those of *R. thomsonii*, there is really no difference. Owing to this early growth it is useless in colder districts and should never be attempted.

R. thomsonii, a blood-red rhododendron, is one of the best known of all with its smooth brown branches, orbicular smooth green leaves and lovely deep blood-red flowers with their prominent calyces. It flowers a little later than *R. meddianum*, at the end of April or early May, and is satisfactory in all districts, but in colder areas it takes more years to flower freely.

A word of warning should be given. When it does flower freely it uses up an enormous amount of energy and soon begins to go back. Advice is often given to dead-head all plants of *R. thomsonii* as soon as they have finished flowering. That may or may not be necessary, but what is important is that it should be fed every year, alternating between mulches of leaf-mould and a good layer of old and well-rotted dung. Rhododendrons with smooth bark such as *R. thomsonii* and *R. barbatum* very rarely produce new growth from old wood. Thus they cannot be pruned, and if a branch is broken or dies back an ugly gap is left. It is so lovely that its good health is worth a deal of effort. One of the latest introductions of *R. thomsonii* by Ludlow and Sherriff is proving too tender for colder districts.

There are two anomalous plants in the series that are given subseries to themselves. The first is *R. cerasinum*, a plant lying between the *Thomsonii* and *Souliei* subseries. It is a medium-sized shrub up to 10 feet, with much narrower leaves than is usual in the series, up to 4 inches long and $1\frac{1}{2}$ inches wide. The pendulous truss carries five to seven flowers up to 2 inches long and campanulate in shape. Like so many of the series it varies in colour from scarlet, or creamy white with a cherry-red band round the edge, to a translucent claret-colour. We have never seen one that is not attractive. In the south it flowers at the end of April, but in Perthshire it is in May. The new growth comes later and is never cut.

This is a first-class garden plant with sufficient colour variation to take the place of *R. cyanocarpum*, *R. eclecteum* and *R. stewartianum* in colder gardens.

The other anomalous species is the well-known dwarf *R. williamsianum*. It is a spreading shrub, never more than 3 feet high and sometimes as much as 5 or 6 feet in diameter. The leaves are rounded, $1\frac{1}{2}$ inches across. Apart from stature the great difference is that there are only two or three flowers in the truss. They are bell-shaped, pale rose with spots. There are so-called red forms, but we have never seen one that is really red except in the bud, and this fades to a somewhat dark rose when the flowers are mature. Their beauty is enhanced by the contrast with the delicate brown of the young foliage which often comes out about the same time.

This lovely plant flowers in April, and both the flowers and young foliage are often cut. Gardeners in the south are usually told to grow it in a sheltered position in at least half-shade. Our oldest plant is in such a situation above a stream and is 3 or 4 feet across, but it is often cut and rarely flowers freely. Another younger plant we have planted in a much colder situation, sheltered from the wind but in three-quarters sun ; it appears to prefer this treatment, does not come into flower or growth so early and sets more flower-buds. We doubt, therefore, if the coddling recommended in the south is good advice for colder areas.

Its quality and character are such that all gardeners should experiment until they can find the treatment best suited for their neighbourhood.

Trichocladum series

This is a series of deciduous or semi-deciduous shrubs, not so very far removed from an azalea. With one exception all that are in cultivation are closely related with much the same behaviour and habit. Except for their height if you have one, you have them all. Of those that are so much alike we would choose *R. melinanthum*, one of the tallest in the series, a deciduous shrub of about 6 feet with glaucous, narrowly obovate leaves 1½ inches long and precocious yellow flowers, four in a truss, very flat-faced, about 1 inch across, but a good clear yellow. We have grown this plant for a number of years and find it quite hardy. It flowers in May.

While some of the other species are quite pretty, care

Trichocladum series : R. melinanthum
(*two-thirds natural size*)

should be taken in their selection, as the quality of the yellow colour varies. They should all be grown in very moderate shade, as they tend to become leggy if kept too dark.

The exception is one of the most lovely of all rhododendrons in foliage. This is *R. lepidostylum*, a spreading rounded bush, not more than 1½ feet in height but often 4 or 5 feet across. It is more evergreen than most of the series, but the young foliage comes out a lovely blue-green tint, quite distinct from the colour of any other rhododendron leaf, and it holds this colour for most of the season. Only towards winter does it tone down to a darker green. The flowers, that come in May or June, are pale yellow, and not of much importance as they often appear within the young foliage. In the north *R. lepidostylum* should be grown in at least three-quarters sun, but it should be sheltered from cold winds. In other respects it is quite hardy. Another new species might be placed in this series. This is *R. cowanianum* from 12,000 feet in Nepal, deciduous, with reddish-purple, not yellow, flowers. There are also differences in the scales. Seedlings are now in cultivation, but nothing is known of its behaviour.

Triflorum series

This is one of the most useful series for the ordinary garden, as it lacks the rather bulky appearance of most of the larger rhododendrons, and is light and airy. This is also enhanced when the plants are in flower, as they are among the most free-flowering of all species and show off their wide-open five-lobed flowers extremely well. On the other hand it is a series about which the gardener has to be careful, as many of the species show variation and some of the colour forms are not nearly so good as others. Luckily in this case this variation is not so much of a gamble. Most if not all root readily from cuttings, and so vegetative reproduction of good clones is fairly rapid, as they grow quite quickly and flower at a moderately young stage. But intending purchasers from nurserymen should make certain that what they are buying is vegetatively produced from these good clones and not an unflowered seedling.

With variable species like these it would appear that far too many varieties have been named as separate species, nor is there any clear distinction between some of the subseries into which they have been divided. For the purpose of this book, therefore, we are dividing them into colour groups.

And we are only mentioning those which are generally in cultivation.

Blues, lavenders and lilacs

R. augustinii is probably the best blue species in existence today in its superior forms. The term blue must, of course, be qualified. Even in its best colours it cannot approach a gentian blue, but both the dark and paler forms are a good lavender blue, pure and with no hint of magenta in them. It is a shrub of ten to twelve feet, with sharply pointed leaf-buds and thin-textured lanceolate leaves, sharply acuminate at the apex and narrowing at the base, about three inches long and barely one inch wide. The flowers are carried three in a truss, about two inches long, widely funnel-shaped with five deeply cut lobes and prominently exserted stamens. Both the leaves and the flowers are very typical of the series. It flowers in early May, a little later in the north.

There are various forms of this charming plant. The deeper blue is unfortunately only hardy in the west and south-west. It is sufficiently tender for it not even to be attempted in colder districts. But we have grown and flowered the less-dark form for a number of years, even in a fairly exposed position. Unless there is a sudden May frost it is perfectly happy. It is in the less-dark forms that there is most colour variation. Some are almost grey lavender, attractive but not so striking as those with brighter tints.

R. chasmanthum is very close to *R. augustinii* with the same colour range. It flowers ten days later than the latter. Apart from the fact that the leaves are usually larger we find it very difficult to tell the difference between them in gardens. It is said to be more tender, but we have had no personal experience. Except that it prolongs the flowering time, we doubt if there is any reason to grow both species even in the most sheltered garden.

R. *zaleucum* is one of the most beautiful in the series but is unfortunately one of the least hardy. It is tall-growing and will reach twenty feet or more. The leaves are typical *triflorum* shape, but they are so glaucous below as to be almost white, while the upper surface is a dark green. The flowers are borne in the usual truss of three to four flowers, but they are larger and the lobes are not so deeply cut. The colour is a good clear lilac, or it may be much paler or almost white, flowering at the end of April. This is unfortunately a definitely tender plant, as it comes into growth too early, but no garden in the west should be without it.

Yellow shades

R. *ambiguum* is a shrub that will reach 6 or 7 feet with leaves that are more rounded at the base than others of the series, 2 to 3 inches long and about 1 inch wide. It produces a truss of three to four flowers 1½ inches long, widely funnel-shaped as usual, pale yellow spotted with green. It flowers in May.

This is a hardy yellow and as such is useful in colder gardens where the early flowering R. *lutescens* is almost invariably cut. But the colour is not so good, as it is inclined to be greenish in tone or so pale as to look more like a dirty white. In its better forms it is a good plant for mixing with R. *augustinii*.

R. *hanceanum* is a dwarf plant described as 3 feet in height but we have never seen it much more than 1½ feet, with leaves more obovate than in most of the series up to 2½ inches long and 1½ inches wide. The truss is more like a raceme and carries six to eight flowers about 1 inch long, a clear pale yellow, in April.

There is a so-called variety *nanum* which may or may not be smaller than the type, but in any case it is a first-class plant for the rock garden when grown in half-shade, free-flowering and surprisingly hardy.

Another low-compact shrub of some value in the rock garden is *R. keiskei* from Japan. The leaves are narrower and more pointed, 2 inches long and ¾ inch wide. The truss is more compact with three to five flowers, a good lemon-yellow and without any spots. Flowering in March in the south and April in the north it is sometimes cut, but it is hardier than one would imagine. It is also free-flowering and with us does not mind almost full sun. The fault is that the texture of the flowers is paper-thin. Thus even in good weather they only last a very few days.

R. lutescens is the finest of the yellows, a shrub up to 6 feet high, with pale primrose-yellow flowers, but unfortunately it is so early flowering, even in February if there is a mild fortnight during the month, that it is a useless luxury in colder gardens. It is not a heavily foliaged plant, but the colour of the leaves is a pleasant lightish-green while the young shoots are bronzed. The loose truss carries three to six flowers 1½ inches across. It is particularly free-flowering, and the flowers do not all come out at once. We have grown it in our cold neighbourhood, but do so no longer, as it is so invariably damaged by frost.

R. triflorum is an 8-foot shrub with mahogany-coloured peeling bark. The leaves are typical and the three-flowered truss is light yellow. We have never seen a clear yellow in its flowers ; it is always either greenish or rather dirty looking. Some authorities praise it for its bark. We grow one or two forms, but we would leave it alone. There is a so-called mahogany form with a mahogany-brown blotch to the flowers.

Whites

R. caeruleum in its typical form is a deep rose-lavender or pale lilac of not great importance, but plants raised from number Rock 59207 have almost all turned out to have lovely white flowers, and it has been called *R. caeruleum album*. This is a smaller plant, about 5 feet in height, with small leaves rather more obtuse at both ends, about $1\frac{1}{2}$ inches long and $\frac{1}{2}$ inch wide. The flowers, three to four in a truss, are small, about $\frac{3}{4}$ inch long, greenish-white in the bud, opening pure white with chocolate spots. It flowers in May, and is hardy under almost any conditions. In habit it is rather like a small edition of *R. augustinii*.

R. *chartophyllum* is a shrub near *R. yunnanense*, but stiffer in its growth. Botanically it only differs in the absence of bristles on the upper surface of the leaves, but in cultivation it is difficult to tell them apart in the normal form. But there is a white form of *R. chartophyllum* that we have grown for many years and would not be without. It is pure white with an orange blotch, and is very hardy and free-flowering, a week or two earlier than *R. yunnanense*.

There is one other difference. *R. chartophyllum* sometimes is almost deciduous, in which case it is called *R. chartophyllum praecox*. In other cases it is semi-deciduous, but is rarely completely evergreen. For instance our white-flowered plant almost always sheds most of its old leaves just before the young leaf buds begin to show green. It is sometimes stated that it is not so good as many others in the series. With this we disagree. It is an excellent garden plant.

Still another species which has a white-flowered form is
R. searsiae. This is a shrub of 4 or 5 feet with leaves 3
inches long and only ¾ inch wide. The truss is three- to four-
flowered. The flowers are either white or mauve, and have
very short pedicels giving a rather more compact truss. It
is a little earlier in flower. Our judgment of it would be
that it is neat but not gaudy.

Pink and Mauve

Real pinks with no hint of mauve are rarities in this series.
The only one to pass the test with flying colours would, in our
opinion, be the best pink forms of *R. davidsonianum*, which are
not only a clear pink but have attractive red spots. The best
form that we know was raised at Headfort in Eire, and this
clone is now being slowly distributed. It flowers in late April
or early May and is one of the most attractive pinks in the
garden.

R. davidsonianum is a rather leggy plant, very like *R. yunnanense* in growth with small bright-green leaves, of the usual
size and shape. The trusses with three to six flowers are
both terminal and axillary. We find it very hardy. In
addition it flowers as a comparatively young plant.

R. exquisitum is a 6-foot relative of *R. oreotrephes* with
glaucous and much more oblong leaves rounded at both ends.
The flowers are a very uncommon shade among rhododendrons, a greyish-mauve without, or with a minimum of,
spots. They are very flat faced, and hold themselves well.
It is quite hardy, flowers in May and is a first-class plant.

R. oreotrephes is one of the most popular species in the
series. It will reach 8 feet. The leaves are oblong,
equally rounded at both ends, about 2 inches long and
barely 1 inch broad, smooth and dark green above, very

glaucous below. The truss has five to eight flowers, neat and not too lax. The flowers are 1½ inches wide, mauve or a mauve-pink, both of which suit the foliage. The colour combination is charming. It is May-flowering.

We have found *R. oreotrephes* a 'choosy' plant. Some have done well and flower freely ; others have disliked where we placed them. Some gardeners in the south have also found it a little difficult. It is not a question of hardiness. Undoubtedly, as Rothschild has remarked, it dislikes moving more than most rhododendrons. It should be planted in its final position as young as possible. *R. oreotrephes* is worth any amount of trouble. We grow it in half-shade, but we do not think this is so important as absence of cold wind, which undoubtedly affects it. It is a variable plant in size of truss, size and shape of flower and colour.

R. artosquameum is very similar, but the colour is a darker rose with no markings and there are fewer flowers in the truss.

R. yunnanense is the most good-tempered plant in the series and should be in every garden. It grows up to 12 feet and sends out leggy branches. This, indeed, is its only fault, as it does make a rather untidy bush. The leaves are the usual *triflorum* shape 2½ inches long, about 1 inch broad. The rather looser truss has three to five flowers, pale or medium-pink, usually with red spots. It flowers in May.

This is one of the most free-flowering of all rhododendron species under almost any conditions. We have one or two plants in quite deep shade, and they seem to flower as freely as others in more sun. When young it is advisable to watch its growth and check any long young growths that may spoil its shape if left to grow uncurbed.

Magentas and Purples

R. concinnum is one of the difficult colours to describe and to place. Like others it is an accumulation of species. It is a shrub about seven feet high with stiffer branches. The leaves are similar to others in the series, but the scales on both surfaces give them a rather duller appearance. The truss is three-flowered. There are two good colour forms ; the rest are unimportant. The first is that which used to be called *R. benthamianum,* a shade of deep blue-violet from which the violet slowly fades leaving a deep lavender blue. The other is called *R. pseudoyanthinum* with reddish-purple flowers, not so much blue as a hot magenta, a wonderful colour when seen with the sun behind it.

Both flower with us in May, and a little earlier in the south. We find them extremely hardy, but care must be taken in both cases to keep them away from pinks and scarlets. They make an admirable combination with *R. wardii.* Don't be put off by the rather uncommon shades, as in their best forms they are first-class garden plants. Naturally they must be vegetatively produced from good-coloured clones.

The last we shall mention in the series is *R. villosum.* This is taller growing and more straggly in growth, and much more hairy both in the young shoots and the leaves. The truss is three-flowered and the colour is usually a bright magenta-purple, not so attractive as that of *R. pseudoyanthinum.* But there is a form, though rare, with deep-purple flowers, almost a royal purple, which is much better, although again it is difficult to place. It is very free-flowering in May.

Uniflorum series

This is an attractive group of dwarf plants fairly close to the *Lepidotum* series. As is obvious from the name, all the plants are either single, or at the most two-flowered.

R. *imperator* is a dwarf, often prostrate, shrub with lanceolate leaves up to 2 inches long and under ½ inch wide. The flowers are narrowly funnel-shaped, 1½ inches long, and surprisingly large for the size of the plant. It also produces flowers at a very young age. It is May-flowering. The colour is a pinkish-purple. The plant is quite hardy, but not always easy to establish ; and it does not seem to like too much shade. R. *patulum* only differs in the arrangement of the scales, so if you have one, you do not want the other.

R. *ludlowii* is a dwarf shrub that appears to be more spreading in cultivation than it is in the wilds. The leaves are obovate and only ½ inch long. The flowers are campanulate, about 1 inch long, yellow spotted with reddish-brown inside the tube. It is May-flowering. This is an attractive little plant, as the flowers stand up well above the foliage. It is quite hardy but very slow growing and not very easy. The best plant we know is in Mr R. B. Cooke's garden in Northumberland.

R. *pemakoense* is an erect or semi-erect shrub up to 1 foot, bushy and neat in habit. The leaves are obovate with a rounded apex up to 1 inch long and ½ inch wide. The flowers are widely funnel-shaped, pinkish-purple. This is very free-flowering, and all the flowers come out at once. This is a disadvantage in a cold garden, as it flowers in April and both the opening buds and the flowers are very frost-tender. For a frost-free garden it is admirable, but our plants

Uniflorum series : R. pemakoense
(two-thirds natural size)

are frosted two years out of three and its value to us is doubtful.

A dwarf form is listed, but we can find no difference between it and the normal one. *R. pemakoense* is very close to *R. uniflorum*, again only differing in the arrangement of the scales, but *R. uniflorum* flowers a week or two later, which is an advantage.

R. pumilum is a dwarf prostrate shrub, growing 2 or 3 inches and then sending out prostrate side branches, and not exceeding 6 inches. The ½-inch leaves are narrower than others in the series. There are occasionally three flowers in the truss ; they are bell-shaped, ½ inch long, rather hairy, and either a clear pink or rose in colour. It is quite hardy and flowers early in May. The true species is uncommon.

Virgatum series : R. racemosum
(two-thirds natural size)

Virgatum series

This is a small series which all produce axillary flower-buds.
R. oleifolium is an erect-growing shrub up to 4 or 5 feet
with 2-inch leaves lanceolate and narrow, only ½ inch wide.
The flowers are almost always single, funnel-shaped about
1 inch long and pubescent on the outside. The colour is
usually pink and occasionally almost white. It flowers in
April. It is a good plant for the west with its fairly large
flowers, but is too tender for cold gardens.

    R. racemosum is possibly the best-known species now grow-
ing in gardens. It is a variable plant. The well-known dwarf
form under Forrest number 19404 remaining about two feet
in height, but we have earlier Forrest plants that are more

than eight feet in height, and very erect-growing. The leaves are wider than in *R. oleifolium* and glaucous below. The axillary trusses are more than single-flowered. They are rather smaller and are not pubescent outside.

This is extremely free-flowering, and most forms will resist a degree or two of frost while in flower. The flowering time varies from early April to mid-May according to the variety. The dwarf form is so popular that the taller-growing varieties are often ignored. To us this is a mistake. We have a six-foot plant with bright-pink flowers that is as good in colour as the dwarf variety, and a group is extremely handsome.

R. virgatum is similar to *R. oleifolium* with larger leaves. It is often reported to be tender and inferior to the others, but it has been a success for years in the rock garden at the Royal Botanic Garden, Edinburgh. There both the pink and the good white forms make upright shrubs of about three feet. It is obviously hardier than *R. oleifolium*.

Azaleas

ONE of the more difficult questions to answer is what is the difference between a rhododendron and an azalea. In the days of Linnaeus *Azalea* was a genus by itself; now it is the *Azalea* series of the genus *Rhododendron*. There are deciduous rhododendrons and evergreen azaleas. Unfortunately the main differences between the two are botanical and do not explain why an azalea looks like an azalea and a rhododendron looks like a rhododendron. The main differences are that an azalea never has scales on its leaves, and almost always has what are called strigose hairs. Strigose hairs are those which are sufficiently stiff to stand out horizontally from the leaf-surface. In most cases the foliage is deciduous, but in the *Obtusum* subseries it is more or less persistent.

Among many rhododendron enthusiasts the azalea is little more than a becoming addition to the main garden scheme, a useful plant that is usually full of flower at its proper season and gives very little trouble. Actually there are few shrubs with a more interesting history, or where so much has been accomplished in improvement with so little publicity.

What is seldom realised is that almost all azaleas, whether species or hybrid, are long-lived plants. Thus they deserve more attention than most gardeners are accustomed to give them. There are plants of both Ghent and Mollis hybrids and also of species in gardens both in the British Isles and in the United States that are well over a hundred years old, and are still magnificent specimens, while in the southern

United States there are hybrids of *R. simsii* well over a century old, which still show no signs of having reached their climacteric.

There is no doubt that the azalea is increasing in general popularity, but the trend is definitely towards hybrids of either old or modern generations and away from the species. In a way this is not surprising, as the nomenclature of the so-called species is extremely involved, and there is little doubt that many of the series are still in a state of flux, and have not yet settled down to genuine specific rank. A case in point is the well-known *R. calendulaceum* of the eastern United States from which so many of the well-known Ghent hybrids have sprung. This shows so many variations in chromosome numbers that many botanists have now come to the conclusion that *R. calendulaceum* itself is no more than a natural hybrid.

The *Azalea* series is divided into six subseries, of which four are important : (1) subseries *Luteum*, deciduous with large flowers which include the parents of our best-known deciduous hybrids ; (2) subseries *Obtusum*, which includes all the evergreen azaleas ; (3) subseries *Schlippenbachii*, an Asiatic group of deciduous species, large flowered with long tubes and leaves in whorls at the end of the stem ; and (4) subseries *Canadense*, deciduous with bell-shaped flowers rather than those with long tubes. There are two subseries with single species ; subseries *Nipponicum* of little or no garden importance and subseries *Tashiroi*, which is not in cultivation.

Azalea series : Luteum subseries

This contains the best-known species of azalea grown in the British Isles, *R. luteum* or *R. flavum* or *Azalea pontica*, the only azalea found in Asia Minor and the lands surrounding the

Black Sea. Its pure yellow, sweetly scented flowers are to be found in countless gardens, but often, oddly enough, more or less by mistake. For many years the Dutch have used it as a stock on which to graft hybrid azaleas. These stocks frequently sucker, and if not watched, the suckers become dominant and in time smother the grafts. In their place have grown larger and stronger plants of *R. luteum*, in much the same way as suckers of *R. ponticum* have killed out thousands upon thousands of old hybrid rhododendrons. It is owing to this suckering propensity that *R. luteum* is so often seen growing where its size and straggling habits are not in keeping with its surroundings. In its place there should obviously be growing smaller and more compact hybrids.

On the other hand *R. luteum* is not used often enough on the edges of woodland where its lovely yellow flowers, delicious scent and good autumn colour can often improve a dark corner.

By far the greatest number of species in this subseries are natives of the United States. As they are complex and complicated, we have thought it better to chart them in alphabetical order with their habitat, habit, colour and scent (see page 152).

The two Asiatic members of this subseries are *R. molle* and *R. japonicum*. As a species the former is of little importance in the British Isles, as it is far from vigorous and is very liable to damage by spring frosts. Its scentless yellow flowers with a greenish blotch are attractive. It seems doubtful if its main claim to fame as one of the parents of the hybrid Mollis azaleas now holds good, It is so tender that it might be presumed that a mistake was made by early hybridists, who had mistaken *R. japonicum* for *R. molle*.

R. japonicum might be called the Japanese equivalent of

Species of American Azaleas

Name	Habitat	Habit	Colour	Scent
alabamense	central-southern U.S.	3–5-feet ; almost always stoloniferous ; dry area	white	lemon
arborescens	Pennsylvania to Alabama	tall and upright ; very hardy ; late flowering	white, style usually red	heliotrope
atlanticum	eastern-central coast	low-growing ; very stoloniferous ; damp situations	white, often flushed pink	aromatic trace of Bog-myrtle
austrinum	south-eastern U.S.	almost the U.S. equivalent of *R. luteum* ; moderately hardy	yellow to orange	variable
calendulaceum	Pennsylvania to Ohio	upright and tall ; almost certainly a natural hybrid	large range from yellow to blood-orange	only moderately scented
canescens	south-east coast of U.S.	very tall ; the most tender of the subseries ; *roseum* is a better garden plant	pale pink	honey-suckle
cumberlandense	Kentucky	not tall, 3–5 feet ; late flowering ; like smaller *prunifolium* ; quite hardy	orange to rich red	very little
nudiflorum	Massachusetts to North Carolina	4–6 feet ; inclined to be stoloniferous ; very hardy ; *speciosum* is sometimes listed as a form	usually pale pink with deeper tube	sweet, not aromatic
oblongifolium	Texas	near *viscosum* ; probably not in the British Isles	white	clove
occidentale	western U.S. sea-board	equivalent of *calendulaceum* ; tall ; late	almost all azalea colours	very sweet
prunifolium	Georgia to Alabama	tall, more spreading large flowers ; late	reddish-orange	medium
roseum	north and north-east U.S.	medium height, upright very hardy	pink	clove
serrulatum	south eastern U.S.	tall ; small-flowered ; *viscosum* is better	white	very sweet
viscosum	eastern U.S.	tall and upright, damp situations ; very hardy	white or pale pink	strong spicy

R. calendulaceum and *R. occidentale*, but the tube is shorter and the flowers are carried in a slightly tighter truss. The colour is equally variable, from yellow through orange to a rich orange-red. Unlike *R. molle* it is sweetly scented. It has certainly been used in the making of Mollis hybrids. One point of difference between it and the American species is that *R. japonicum* will grow under less acid conditions.

While most of the azaleas in this subseries are attractive plants, they hybridise very freely with anything within range. The difficulty is in finding those which are true to type. Azalea authorities in the United States have described how one species runs into the next almost the length and breadth of the country, with the exception of *R. occidentale* on the west coast. Thus, even if seed is collected in the wild, it is almost impossible to guarantee that it is true to type.

Azalea series : Schlippenbachii subseries

All the species in this subseries are Asiatic, and they all have large flowers. Leaves appear in whorls at the end of the shoots, and terminal buds produce both flowers and leaf-shoots. The type species is one of the best of all azaleas. It makes a densely branched, widely spreading shrub, eight or ten feet high and as much through. The flowers come out in May at the same time as the leaves and are as much as four inches across. The colour is white or pale pink or a rich deep pink. It comes from Korea and Manchuria and is quite hardy.

R. reticulatum is an alliance of several species, among them *R. rhombicum* and *R. dilatatum*. It is tall and erect-growing, with flowers appearing before the leaves in April. The lobes of the corolla are divided almost down to the base. The colour is reddish-purple. This is a very free-flowering azalea, and the colour is not so unattractive as it sounds ; but it flowers too early for colder districts. The leaves colour well in autumn.

R. quinquefolium is equally tall-growing and erect. The colour of the flowers is pure white with greenish dots. While this is also good in autumn, it is too shy of flowering in this country to be of great horticultural value.

R. weyrichii is more tree-like in growth, particularly in its form *amagianum*. The flower colour is difficult to describe. Here are a few sample descriptions : red, orange-red with purple blotch, bright pink suffused mauve, or brick-red. They are about 2½ inches across. In the form *amagianum* the flowers are larger and appear in July instead of April/May.

Canadense subseries

In this subseries the new shoots spring from buds below the terminal bud, and, in the two American species, *R. canadense* and *R. vaseyi*, the two lower lobes of the corolla are larger and more clearly divided from the upper lobes. This gives the flowers a light and graceful appearance.

R. canadense, often called *Rhodora canadense*, an upright and very twiggy shrub, is rarely more than three feet tall. It has grey-green leaves and rose-purple flowers about one inch in diameter. There is also a white form, a charming plant. This is another of those rhododendrons that succeeds better in colder areas. When flowering well it is an attractive plant, but a little uninteresting at other times. It will grow under wetter conditions than most of the genus and likes a very acid soil. It is April-flowering.

R. vaseyi comes from farther south in the eastern United States, but is equally hardy and is a better garden plant. It is a tall and upright grower and will reach ten or more feet in cultivation. The flowers are usually a pale rose-pink, and also white, with a greenish throat and orange-red spots. A first-class plant.

R. albrechtii from Japan is rather like a smaller form of *R. schlippenbachii*, with 2-inch flowers of deep rose in the end of April. We have no experience of this plant, but others tell us that it is none too easy.

The fourth species in the subseries, *R. pentaphyllum*, also from Japan, with an inflorescence of only one or two flowers of a bright rose-pink, may be worth all the praise it is given in one or two gardens, but generally it is a very shy flowerer.

Azalea series : Obtusum subseries

This subseries contains about thirty species, most of which are evergreen, but some have persistent leaves. This means that the larger leaves may shrivel and drop off, but smaller leaves will remain until the next crop of new leaves appears. Of these thirty species a number are not in cultivation. Of those that remain several have been cultivated by the Japanese for centuries, and numerous colour forms exist which are really selections of the species and not necessarily hybrids. These in turn have been increased by vegetative means, and are really clones of selected forms that may have been grown in Japan for generations. Typical of this form are the Kurume azaleas, of which many are colour forms of *R. obtusum* var. *japonicum*.

These evergreen azaleas are made more complicated by the fact that the various strains of popular greenhouse plants that first became fashionable almost a hundred years ago, and most of which were raised in Belgium, are commonly called Indian azaleas. No azaleas are known in India, nor have they arisen from *R. indicum*, which itself is a plant from southern Japan, not from India, but from *R. simsii*, a species which is widespread in various forms throughout southern China and as far west as Upper Burma.

Thus from a garden point of view the subseries contains a number of species of all of which a number of forms exist, varying from the absolutely hardy to greenhouse plants. Hybrids between them will be mentioned later.

R. indicum from southern Japan is one of the hardier evergreens. They are useful as they are late-flowering. The type is fairly erect but with stiff branches and a one- to two-flowered inflorescence, the flowers being 2 inches in diameter, red or rose-red or scarlet ; June-flowering. There are two forms in cultivation outside Japan, and many more waiting to be introduced. The two forms are var. *balsaminæflorum*, a dwarfer bush with semi-double salmon-rose flowers, and var. *crispiflorum*, better known under its old name *macrantha* with bright-pink flowers and wavy petals.

While these and other late-flowering azaleas are never damaged by spring frosts, we have found that in colder districts they sometimes fail to ripen the tips of their current year's growth, and these may be damaged by autumn frosts. They should always be grown in full sun, at least in colder districts.

R. linearifolium var. *macrosepalum* is one of the species from Japan that is partly deciduous. It is very variable in size and in the number of flowers, but the leaves are always under $\frac{1}{2}$ inch wide and about $2\frac{1}{2}$ inches long. The colour of the flowers is pale mauve with a darker eye, sweetly scented and flowering in June. The type is a cultivated Japanese form with strap-shaped petals, more peculiar than beautiful.

R. mucronatum is an old favourite under its more popular

name *Azalea ledifolia*. This is almost evergreen, much branched and wide-spreading. The flowers are either single or up to three in a truss, about two inches across, pure white, flowering at the end of May. There is a slightly larger form, called Bulstrode, with a pale greenish-yellow eye. We also remember years ago a fine form called *Noordtianum* which often had white flowers striped rose, but we have not seen it listed for years. These are among the hardiest of all ever-green azaleas, and are charming if grown in thin woodland, but they should not be grown in deep shade.

R. obtusum is the name given to an alliance of Japanese species or varieties, all of which come from the uplands in western China and take the place of our heather or the *Lapponicum* series. As we mentioned before, var. *japonicum* (probably better called var. *kiusianum* to save confusing it with *R. japonicum* the parent of many of the Mollis azaleas) is the fountain-head of many of the Kurume azaleas, always round bushy plants that will reach not more than three feet. Typical varieties are Azuma Kagami, deep pink, hose-in-hose; Hino Degiri, bright crimson; Kirin, deep silvery-rose; Kure-no-yuke, white, hose-in-hose; and Rasho-Mon, scarlet.

While these Kurume azaleas are called perfectly hardy, they must have ample sunshine if they are to flower regularly and freely. They are excellent plants for the southern half of England, but for the north and Scotland they are not perfect, although they will flower freely after a hot summer and autumn. In any case they are better grown in full sun.

The variety *amoenum* is near to var. *kiusianum* with the same small flowers, but it is on the whole a taller plant, with its branches spreading in definite tiers. The type is a not very attractive magenta, but in old gardens, particularly in the south of England, there are large plants of better-coloured varieties. At Wisley and at Exbury there are very large plants, ten or more feet across and five feet high. On the whole, however, the various forms of *amoenum* have been superseded, although we personally think their tiered shape most attractive. Some authorities place the well-known Hi-no-Mayo in this group, but it more properly belongs to the Kurumes.

The variety *kaempferi* is a much larger plant which will reach 10 feet, with flowers varying from $1\frac{3}{4}$ inches to $2\frac{1}{2}$ inches across. The colour is salmon-red to deep pink. This is a magnificent plant in thin woodland in the south, but again should be grown in more sun the farther north it is planted, if it is to flower freely.

There is a dwarfer form called Mikado which flowers very late, and in the United States a clone has been found, called Indian Summer, which flowers in October. This might be a useful plant to introduce to Cornish and West of Scotland gardens.

The fourth variety of *R. obtusum* is called *macrostemon* with smaller flowers, $1\frac{1}{2}$ inches in diameter, bright salmon-orange, with long exserted stamens. This is very low-growing and is seldom more than 1 foot high. It also is very late in flowering and is useful as a hardy plant.

R. oldhamii is a tender azalea, tall and much branched, from Formosa. The evergreen leaves are pale green and thickly covered with rust-coloured hairs. The flowers are brick-red and come out in May. This is a lovely plant but too tender for normal use even in the west. It has, however, been used with great success at Exbury as a parent of some first-class evergreen hybrids.

R. scabrum is a plant from the Liukiu Islands off Japan,

and is also found in Okinawa. It is a lax-growing shrub up to six feet, with large evergreen leaves and a two- to six-flowered truss with flowers rose-red to rich scarlet in the form *coccineum*. It flowers in April/May and is definitely tender. This is a pity as it is one of the most striking of all azaleas, with flowers often four inches across. In Japan and the United States it has been and is being used freely as a parent but its value as a parent has been neglected in this country. It has been used by Wada as a parent for some of his finest evergreen hybrids. It has also been grown under the name *sublanceolatum*.

R. serpyllifolium is deciduous, low-growing and much branched, with tiny leaves not more than $\frac{1}{2}$-inch long and flowers no more than 1 inch across, rosy pink, or white in the form *albiflorum*. This charming little plant flowers in late April, or May farther north. It is one of those plants that is really more satisfactory in the south of England, although we have grown it in the 1930s for a number of years. It was often cut. We have not replaced it, but if we lived in the south we would certainly grow it.

R. simsii an evergreen azalea from south China, grows about five to eight feet and has rose-red to dark red-spotted flowers. It is extremely tender, and in the British Isles can only be grown as a greenhouse plant. It is the parent of most of the evergreen greenhouse azaleas.

There is a form, however, called *eriocarpum*, which is much hardier, comes into flower in June and July, and into growth in July and August. These are the charming Gumpo azaleas, evergreen, very low and spreading, rarely more than six to eight inches high, with large flowers. There are about six different colours, ranging from white, through pink to a darkish red. In the north they require a little cover during a very cold spell, but in the south where the young wood ripens fully before autumn frosts they are almost completely hardy, much more so than the newer Wada hybrids. As it is a question of wood ripening before winter sets in, they should be grown in a sheltered place in the north, in almost full sun.

R. yedoense var. *poukhanense* from Korea is partly deciduous. It is a compact thickly branched shrub of three feet, or six feet if grown in shade. The truss is two- to three-flowered with two-inch flowers rose to pale lilac and fragrant. It is May-flowering. This is one of the hardiest of this subseries, and an excellent plant. *R. yedoense* itself is a completely double form long grown in Japan usually pale rose-purple with a fairly large calyx.

Hybrid Azaleas

The azalea has quite rightly been a popular garden flower for more than a hundred years. The deciduous species, as then known, were used extensively to produce various groups of hybrids, which ever since have kept their popularity. At the start the evergreens were limited entirely to plants suitable for the greenhouse and for forcing. In the case of the deciduous hybrids hybridising has been going on ever since. The consequence is that hybrid groups are of extremely mixed parentage, a mixture that is increased when it is remembered that some of the species from the eastern United States are themselves in a state of flux with a preponderance of natural hybrids in large areas where two or more species overlap. A great deal has been written about these hybrid azaleas and their parentage, some of it guess-work, although it is known to a greater degree how the early hybrids were made.

Our personal feeling is that in the past far too many hybrids, obviously very much alike and closely allied, have been named, a practice that is now changing. It has been found that in some cases seedlings, if not exactly true to type, are coming true within certain defined colour ranges, with the consequence that seedlings of pink, or yellow and white, or orange and red shades are now obtainable in the trade. These satisfy all but the most fastidious, and only the most striking advances in the new seedlings are given names.

The following are the most important groups. We have not given individual names, as in many cases the same plant goes under several names both in this country and in the United States.

Ghent Hybrids

The plants are all upright and tall. The flowers are from $1\frac{1}{2}$ to $2\frac{1}{2}$ inches wide, and always have a long tube. They are late-flowering and fragrant. There are both single and double flowers, and the colour range is extremely wide, from white through pale yellow to purple ; and in some cases the primary colour is overlaid with a secondary. In the course of years over 350 varieties have been named.

The first Ghent hybrids appeared in Belgium about 1830 to be followed by English-made hybrids about 1840. At the start the species most often used as parents were *R. luteum*, *R. nudiflorum*, *R. viscosum* and *R. calendulaceum*. Later *R. occidentale* and *R. japonicum* were added among others.

The old-fashioned *Rustica flore pleno* hybrids were produced by crossing double Ghents with Mollis hybrids. They flower in May at the same time as Mollis hybrids.

Still later Anthony Waterer in the Knaphill Nursery developed the Ghent hybrids further, producing magnificent plants with much larger trusses, sometimes carrying up to thirty flowers. The individual flowers are wider and flatter but still with a narrow tube. While many of them carry on the old Ghent habit of tall and upright growth, there is a noticeable change in others to a more dwarf and spreading habit. These Knaphill Azaleas have in turn been used for further sets of hybrids at Exbury, with an even more striking range of colours, if that were possible.

Mollis Hybrids

This race was raised mostly by Anthony Waterer in England and Anthony Koster in Holland in the 1880's. It is usually stated that they have arisen as a cross between *R. molle* and *R. japonicum*, but the former is so tender that it is more likely that many of the early forms were selected seedlings of *R. japonicum* which itself has a wide colour range. They are May flowering.

The flowers are larger with a shorter tube than those of the original Ghents. They are generally supposed not to be so hardy, and that is undoubtedly the case when they are planted in near-zero or sub-zero temperatures, but we have found that they are nearly the same in degree of hardiness as the Ghents provided that they are on their own roots. Whereas Ghents seem to behave in the same fashion whether they are grafted plants or on their own roots, there is no doubt that Mollis hybrids should always be supplied on their own roots. In tests that have been made grafted plants are noticeably less hardy, possibly owing to poor graft unions.

Evergreen Hybrids

With the exception of the greenhouse hybrids, mostly raised in Belgium from 1850 to 1880 between various colour forms and varieties of *R. simsii*, the majority of the evergreen hybrids have not been in cultivation for very long in Europe and the United States

Kurume Hybrids

These are the best known of the evergreen groups of hardy azalea hybrids. As far as is known they were raised in Japan about 1820 from selected forms of their native *R. kiusianum*, possibly with the addition of *R. kaempferi* blood. There are about 300 named clones, and it is obvious that with that number there must be considerable variation in height, size and colour, but as a rule, whatever the size, they are dense in growth and usually spreading. The flowers are either single or hose-in-hose and of every colour except yellow, orange and, of course, blue. They flower in mid-season, between the latter half of April and the end of May.

As mentioned before, these are ideal plants for the south of England, or any climate where there is ample sunshine to bring out the flowers and to ripen the young wood in autumn. In colder districts their value is more doubtful. While undoubtedly hardy, they are often not sufficiently free-flowering, and it is in this that they are supreme in the azalea world when well grown. It would be worth attempting them in greater quantity in such a cold area as our garden in eastern Perthshire, if it were not for the fact that there are other more modern hybrids that are proving to be more free-flowering in our climate, particularly the crosses between *R. kaempferi* and *malvatica* and the new evergreen azaleas recently raised at Exbury, mostly between *R. kaempferi* and *R. oldhamii*. These are all a little more bushy than the Kurumes with larger leaves, but the colour range is equally good and the flowers are larger.

We find that the difficulty with these evergreen azaleas is the danger of their continuing to grow too late in the autumn, with the consequence that young wood is often cut during the following winter. We cannot stress too much the advice to grow them as much as possible in full sun and sheltered from cold winds in northern districts. In warmer climates many of these new evergreen hybrids grow quickly, and end as plants eight or ten feet high. We have seen them that height at Exbury, and they may grow considerably taller.

In the Eastern United States where the winters are too severe for the general run of evergreen hybrids, including the Kurumes, a great deal of hybridising has been going on for the past twenty years, largely by B. Y. Morrison, who has brought out a large range called the Glen Dale hybrids and The Gable hybrids raised by Joseph B. Gable in Pennsylvania. Of the Gable hybrids we have no experience, but we have seen a number of the Glen Dale hybrids, and there is no doubt that there will be a great future in them. They were raised at Glen Dale in Maryland for the Division of Plant Exploration and Introduction of the United States, and are primarily intended as a range that would be hardy in the middle Atlantic states. They are proving satisfactory plants in the home counties, and the south of England, but as far as we know have not been really tested in the colder areas of the British Isles. One factor in their favour is their really extraordinary range, not only of time of flowering but also of colour. In addition to a great range of selfs there are a number of stripes and whites with frilled edges of contrasting colours. On the whole the size of flower is also larger than those of the usual run of evergreen azaleas seen in this country. A representative collection of them is grown at Wisley.

Hybrid Rhododendrons

THE subject of hybrid rhododendrons is a problem. We in Scotland are not so hybrid-minded as many enthusiasts in England. Indeed some of us consider that much of the hybridising that was carried out between the wars, if not entirely without method, was judged through such rosy spectacles that dozens of plants were named and appeared in the rhododendron studbook which should have been left nameless and forgotten. It is true that many have later been ignored and have sunk into oblivion, but their names still clutter up the studbook.

In addition, there is the difficult problem of different forms of well-known hybrids, and, in due course, of their progeny. Under the new international rules of nomenclature their naming is going to be of ever-increasing difficulty. And the same applies to their propagation by the nursery trade, to whom, after all, most of us look for our supply of rhododendrons whether species or hybrids.

We have described earlier how a number of groups within some of the series are still in a state of flux, and how their range of variation shows that they have not yet settled down into their definite grooves and become established species; in other words how they can still be considered as natural hybrids. In turn this means that particularly good varieties within these groups can only be reproduced by vegetative means, if their special characteristics are to be perpetuated.

If this is the case with so-called species that are possibly natural hybrids, how much more so is it with man-made hybrids. There are a few examples, but not very many, where all the progeny of a cross show very little variation, such as that fine hybrid, Polar Bear (*diaprepes* × *auriculatum*), where a large batch was grown at Tower Court, Ascot, all very much alike. At the other extreme we suppose the best-known example is that splendid hybrid between *R. griffithianum* and *R. fortunei*, which is usually called *R. x loderi*, and presumably under the new rules should be called by its prior name *R. x kewense*. It is only natural that *R. x kewense* should differ from *R. x loderi*, as the former was raised at Kew and the latter at Leonardslee from different parents. It is said that the pollen parent, *R. fortunei*, was much superior at Leonardslee. But that is not the whole story. There is great variation among *R. x loderi*, and no less than twenty-three different varieties have been considered sufficiently distinct to be given a varietal name.

While *R. x loderi* may be an extreme example, there are many more. There are ten named varieties of Lady Chamberlain and nine of Naomi, to name only two.

Still further popular species and hybrids have been used as parents *ad infinitum*. In the 1952 *Rhododendron Handbook* *R. campylocarpum* is given as the parent of 43 hybrids, *R. dichroanthum* of 36, *R. discolor* of 37, *R. griersonianum* of no less than 122, *R. griffithianum* of 55 and *R. x loderi* in its various forms of 67.

When totalled the number of rhododendron hybrids is colossal, and it is still increasing. This has not made the task of choosing a reasonable number of good hybrids an easy one.

It must not be thought that we are prejudiced against hybrids ; very far from it, but we have tried to make our choice in a more or less logical way. We have made certain rules, and in almost if not every case, we have made our choice conform to those rules.

The rules run something like this :

I The hybrid must be obtainable in the nursery trade, even if it is not kept by every nursery. It would be ridiculous to suggest a chance-seen hybrid of which possibly only one exists.

II A hybrid is either (A) unlike any other rhododendron in cultivation or (B) like something already in cultivation. If it is (A), it can obviously be included. If it is (B), it would have to be a plant either :

(*a*) with a better habit than anything already existing ; or

(*b*) more easily grown than anything already existing ; or

(*c*) that flowered at a different time ; or

(*d*) that was very much more free-flowering than anything already existing.

After a long life among rhododendrons it is, of course, quite impossible to remember, even if one had seen, all the hybrids which are obtainable in the trade, but we have pooled our memories and have produced a list of hybrids, which no doubt leaves out many worthy plants, but at least gives a beginner something to get his teeth into until he feels able to make a firm choice for himself.

Taller-growing hybrids—Creams and Yellows

Many of these are plants with R. *campylocarpum* as a parent, and it has produced some excellent offspring. Apart from some which are totally different in habit, many are more free-flowering in larger trusses and prolong the flowering season from April until well on in May. These hybrids are particularly useful in colder districts where *R. campylocarpum* itself is what is considered an uncertain plant. It is difficult to make a choice, but ultimately we decided that among ours would be Dairymaid, quite compact in growth and useful for a small garden, flowers pink in the bud opening to a clear yellow with a red blotch, April to May ; Goldsworth Yellow, not quite so compact, apricot in the bud opening to primrose yellow, April to May, one of the most free-flowering of the group ; Unique, again a compact shrub, peach-coloured in the bud, opening to cream with a hint of ochre on red pedicels, a little earlier in flower in the north than the other two. The above three are all plants with more or less the habit of *R. campylocarpum*.

Letty Edwards, a hybrid between *R. campylocarpum* and *R. fortunei*, follows more after the second parent, taller growing with a larger truss and flowers that are not bell-shaped like *R. campylocarpum*. This is a clear yellow, sometimes with a red throat, but all forms are good. It flowers towards the end of April.

We feel that we must include the old Penjerrick, which grows as a small tree. The parentage is *R. griffithianum* and the tall form of *R. campylocarpum* called *elatum*, and it is found in various shades of white, creamy yellow and almost an apricot, also a pale pink with a yellow flush. With that parentage it has a reputation as a tender plant, but we know of two plants growing beautifully in a sheltered corner in a Fife garden ; but it must have complete shelter from cold winds. The flowers are bell-shaped, showing the influence of both parents. It is indeed a lovely plant.

Finally in this group we place Lady Bessborough with

R. discolor as the other parent. This is always a small tree in habit with good foliage. There are various forms, differing mainly in the colour of the flower-buds, which varies from apricot to salmon-pink. When fully opened the colour is cream or creamy yellow with a deep red eye. As might be expected from the parentage, it flowers comparatively late, in May, and is very rarely caught by frost. It is a good colour and a graceful plant.

We must include Idealist in this group, although the parentage is the closely related *R. wardii* and Naomi. This has the bold foliage of the latter parent and the flowers are much wider open in fine trusses, orange-pink in the bud and finally a clear yellow. This prolongs the flowering season a little later in colder districts at a time when yellow-flowered shrubs are not common.

Whites and Creams

It is more difficult to make a choice among the innumerable white or near-white hybrids if the choice is to pass our tests. The first one to pass with flying colours would certainly be Loder's White. This is a plant of good habit, with a large and shapely and upstanding truss, that will stand near zero weather and full sun and wind with equal fortitude ; and, above all, is a great advance on the old cast-iron whites. It never grows out of hand, and so is of great value in gardens where the limit must be a seven- or eight-foot shrub. While it is pink in the bud it soon turns to pure white. It is certainly one of our favourite rhododendrons.

From these we should turn to the white forms of *R. x loderi* among them King George and White Diamond. Is it sacrilege to say that we consider almost all forms of *R. x loderi* vastly overrated, as they are coarse in habit, and loose in truss? If you like a floppy, luscious flower with little symmetry or grace to hold it up, you will rave over *R. x loderi*. We do not. Above all we think that it lacks that indefinable breeding that is to be seen in the more subdued Loder's White and in such charming hybrids as Lady Bessborough and Penjerrick. If you do like something large and gorgeous, there is nothing better than King George and White Diamond among the whites, and Sir Joseph Hooker in the flushed pinks. The variety we like the best is the lovely pale pink called Venus.

R. x loderi grows better in the south and west, and in all cases should be grown in partial shade. We like a newer hybrid with it as one of the parents, the other being *R. calophytum*. This is called Avalanche, white-flushed pink. It is neither so floppy in growth nor in the truss. Its only fault is that it is in flower by the end of March in a forward year, and is sometimes cut by frost.

Another very reliable white hybrid is Mrs Lindsay Smith, very free-flowering with a medium-sized truss, pure white with crimson speckles on the upper petals. It grows to a larger size than Loder's White and flowers at least a fortnight later. Finally we would include that excellent tall-growing Tower Court hybrid called Polar Bear, whose parents are *diaprepes* × *auriculatum*, as in this case it prolongs the flowering time of white rhododendrons until well on in July. It will reach twelve or more feet with handsome foliage. This passes our tests as being a more reliable plant in flower than either of its parents.

Pinks

There is no difficulty about the choice of the earliest pink, as this is Christmas Cheer, a very old hybrid whose parentage is unknown, but undoubtedly with a large admixture of *caucasicum* blood in it. It is low-growing, about three feet tall and spreading, with small trusses opening pink and fading as they grow older. In a mild winter they will really start to open about Christmas-time. One of the great advantages of this plant is that flowers continue to open over a long period. Thus, if the first succession is frosted, there will be dozens of tight buds left that are completely unharmed by the hardest frost so long as they are not showing colour. Even in our cold area we get a succession of flowers for six to eight weeks during any mild weather. The only other hybrid with which it could be confused is Rosa Mundi, but this is taller-growing, the trusses are a little larger and pinker ; and with us it never attempts to open its flowers before the end of February. It does not carry such a long succession of flowers, so is more easily damaged.

For all its flamboyant beauty we still feel that **Pink Pearl** supplies a want that no other rhododendron can fill. It has a large if not refined truss, it will grow under almost any conditions, it is extremely free-flowering, and it does not grow too large. A sport from it, Mother-of-Pearl, with paler buds that open to a creamy white is more charming though not so colourful. A newer hybrid of the same type as **Pink Pearl** which we like is Betty Wormald, deep-pink flowers with a faint purple marking. The above all flower in May and June.

Another old plant that we would not be without is Luscombei, but it should be the Leonardslee variety. The original cross made in 1880 between *R. fortunei* and *R. thomsonii* was a rather hard aniline carmine ; the Leonardslee variety is a softer carmine with a darker throat. This is a tall-growing hybrid, free-flowering, a kind of half-way house between the *thomsonii* and the late hybrids. It flowers in early May. Still another fine old hybrid with the lovely *griffithianum* shape of flower is Cornish Cross, with smooth pale-brown stems and rosy-pink flowers carried in large trusses. Like Penjerrick it must be sheltered from all wind.

Mrs G. W. Leak pink, with a brown-purple blotch, and Mrs Furnival, light pink with a sienna blotch, are the modern equivalents of the old-fashioned blotched hybrids, and are, of course, greatly improved in size of flower and general deportment.

Of the newer pink hybrids probably no modern collection can afford to be without some form or other of Naomi (Aurora × *R. fortunei*). This will form a large and sturdy bush of ten to twelve feet with good foliage. The large sweet-scented flowers vary from pale pink to a rich rose, but always with an undertone of yellow and with more yellow in the throat. It is sufficiently handsome to be grown as a specimen plant in thin woodland. It is May flowering.

Finally there are the hosts of hybrids with *R. griersonianum* as one of the parents, and many of them of almost indescribable colours that run from the oranges and the salmons to the pinks and the reds. Probably many of them are no better than their parent, but there are some that are well worth growing, such as Fabia, orange-salmon with an orange throat, Azor, soft salmon with the added advantage that it does not flower until well on in June, and Vanessa in several forms varying from soft pink to salmon pink and rose pink.

Reds and Scarlets

We are rather more hesitant about one of the earliest red hybrids, *R. x nobleanum*, a cross between *R. caucasicum* and

R. arboreum. It will certainly flower during a mild February, but we find that unlike Christmas Cheer the flowers all tend to open at once. If one is frosted, the whole lot are likely to go. But it is so cheerful with its red-scarlet flowers that we are always ready to take the risk.

The next early red, which we would certainly not be without is *R. x shilsonii* (*thomsonii* x *barbatum.*) Every part of this fine hybrid has character about it, the cinnamon-red bark, the very dark foliage and the shapely bright-red flowers. With us it flowers in March. The trusses last well in water. A little later comes the lovely *R. x barclayi* in early April with its deep blood-red flowers, but this is definitely a more tender plant, really only fit for the milder south and west.

The modern reds and scarlets are much influenced by the use as parents of members of the *Parishii* subseries of the *Irroratum* series, all of which have brilliant red flowers, But it must be remembered that this subseries contains tender plants that can only be grown in the mildest gardens. Although the offspring are certainly hardier, most of them cannot be considered to be hardy hybrids : in other words they must be given shelter and a certain amount of shade. They have one advantage, that many of them flower in late May or June when danger from frost is usually over. But they are not plants for the coldest districts.

We would make a choice from Fusilier or Grenadier, both of which have *R. elliottii* as a parent, the former is a lovely late-flowering scarlet, the latter is much deeper, a rich blood-red, Tally Ho, with *R. eriogynum* as a parent, also a lovely scarlet with a long tube, but in this case it is a rather more tender plant. Even later in June Romany Chal flowers, again with *R. eriogynum* as a parent, with very fine trusses of deep blood-red. Romany Chai with *R. griersonianum* as a parent is similar, with rather paler flowers, and is a slightly lower-growing bush.

One of the finest of the new early flowering reds is Matador, *griersonianum × strigillosum*. The large trusses are a bright scarlet, of a better colour than is usual in *R. strigillosum*, and they last in good condition for a long time, if they are not frosted.

Of all the hybrids of *R. griersonianum* possibly the best for the average garden is May Day, of which the other parent is *R. haematodes*. It flowers in May with large trusses of brilliant scarlet flowers, and forms a bush of not more than six feet. It has the good qualities of both parents, and is a very fine plant. There are many forms.

Finally there are two Dutch hybrids that each fill a particular place in the flowering calendar. The first is Britannia, a low spreading bush with crimson-scarlet flowers in late May, thus coming between the early hybrids and those that flower in June, and the Earl of Athlone with blood-red flowers of good quality that appear two or three weeks earlier. Between them they fill a gap. Britannia is the better-tempered plant, as the Earl of Athlone requires some shelter and feeding if it is not to grow old before its time. Nevertheless it is a lovely colour and is very free-flowering.

Lavenders and Purples

There are not many of the taller hybrids with lavender or purple flowers. The first that always comes to mind is the old *R. fastuosum flore pleno* with its charming flowers of lavender-mauve, sufficiently double from its petaloid stamens, yet without being coarse in any way. As a good tempered and absolutely hardy late-flowering plant it is one of the best.

Possibly hybrid is a wrong term when speaking of this plant, as its origin is unknown. Some go so far as to say that it is a sport of *R. catawbiense*, but that does not detract from its value.

Certainly the best of the larger lavender hybrids is Susan, one of whose parents is certainly *R. campanulatum*, but it is nearer blue than even the best forms of its parent. The foliage is handsome and shows off the large trusses. It flowers usually late in April or early in May.

There are several purple hybrids, all of them made many years ago. The usual choice lies between Purple Splendour and Royal Purple, both of which are good, but we would settle on Purple Splendour as it has a black eye which is more in keeping with its colour than the yellow eye of Royal Purple which we don't think is an improvement.

Cinnabarinum hybrids

Finally among the larger hybrids there is a small group that does not conform to any of our divisions. This consists mostly of two closely allied hybrids in their various forms, Lady Chamberlain and Lady Rosebery. The parentage is *R. cinnabarinum* var. *roylei* and the orange form of Royal Flush in the former, and the pink form in the latter. They have produced lovely hybrids with hanging flowers more like a lapageria than a rhododendron and their texture is waxy. The young growth is glaucous-blue, and the foliage generally is very like that of var. *roylei*. The only difference between the two plants is that the various varieties of Lady Chamberlain vary from apricot through orange-yellow flushed with red to orange-red, while those of Lady Rosebery are rose to delicate pink with no hint of orange.

Both flower in May. We have grown Lady Chamberlain

for a number of years, fairly sheltered and in half-sun. Beyond having the flowers cut by a late May frost, we find it perfectly hardy.

Lower-growing hybrids

It is difficult to draw a definite dividing line between usual garden hybrids and those that might be useful in the rock garden. For instance we find that the old hybrid *R. x praecox* will grow taller than Britannia, but the former has a cloud of neat flowers that fit in with almost any rock-garden scheme, whereas Britannia has large trusses that make it totally unfitted. Thus general appearance has more to do with suitability than actual height.

Blues and near-blues

The colour that has undoubtedly benefited in this class of hybrid is the blue or near-blue. Luckily all these hybrids are easily increased by cuttings, and flower at an early age, as some forms are much better than others. Clonal stocks should always be obtained and not seedlings of these smaller hybrids. For instance Impeanum is a hybrid between *R. impeditum* and *R. hanceanum,* the latter being a dwarf yellow species of the *Triflorum* series. In its best forms, in which *R. impeditum* is obviously the dominant parent, it is a good lilac. Impeanum is lower and more compact than the better-known Blue Tit and Blue Diamond.

Both of these will grow to four feet and more in diameter. They are more complimentary to each other than many gardeners imagine. Blue Tit with us is in full flower a fortnight before Blue Diamond, and the flowers are a slightly paler shade of lavender-blue. Blue Diamond as it opens has almost a purple tinge, but this disappears and a darker and

richer lavender-blue is left. Both are first-class free-flowering
shrubs during the second half of April and the first half of
May with flowers like a smaller edition of *R. augustinii*, but
with us at any rate Blue Diamond carries more flowers each
year than Blue Tit.

Blue Tit has been crossed back again with one of its
parents, *R. impeditum*, and this has produced a smaller and
bluer edition called Sapphire, one of the best dwarf hybrids
that has been raised.

One of the largest of these blue hybrids is Augfast, *fastigiatum × augustinii*. This forms a rounded bush, four feet or more
rather like Blue Tit in shape and colour of flower, but a little
earlier. In a sheltered situation it will flower fairly early in
April.

Red and scarlet hybrids

The value of *R. forrestii* as a parent is now thoroughly realised,
chiefly owing to the production at Bodnant of Elizabeth,
certainly the finest hybrid that has been produced for almost
any garden. It has so much in its favour. The flowers are
large for the size of the plant, and show signs of both parents,
R. forrestii and *R. griersonianum*. The truss of five or six
flowers, each of which is up to three inches across, appears
on a young plant only two or three years old. The colour is
a rich crimson-scarlet.

There are at least two major forms, the one more upright-
growing that will form a bush up to three feet high, with
rather stiff branches, the other much dwarfer and inclined to
creep and spread like *R. forrestii*, and with slightly smaller
flowers of the same colour. This is called Jenny. The general
flowering time starts about the middle of April. It is certainly one of the most free-flowering of all hybrids at an early

age. It is absolutely hardy, but it should not be grown in quite full sun.

The number of hybrids made with *R. forrestii* as a parent is increasing, but none quite come up to the beauty and good temper of Elizabeth. Carmen is a hybrid with *R. didymum*, of the same general habit but smaller, and with crimson flowers almost too dark unless the sun is behind them. Little Ben was one of the first to be made, in this case *R. neriiflorum* is the other parent. It never grows more than two feet high with bright scarlet flowers, but is not quite so free-flowering. Ethel is nearer Elizabeth, but we find it slower-growing. No doubt there will be many more.

Pinks

The great parent for dwarf or semi-dwarf pink hybrids is *R. williamsianum*. Almost all have a rounded bushy habit, with rounded leaves and the bell-shaped flowers of *R. williamsianum*. We have chosen three which differ from each other in a number of points. The first to open in April is Humming Bird, of which the other parent is *R. haematodes*. In this the truss carries four to five flowers, deep pink shaded with a deeper red. Next is Temple Belle, of which the other parent is *R. orbiculare*. In this case the hybrid is closer to the latter than to *R. williamsianum*, and really falls half-way between the two in size, while the colour is almost exactly that of *R. orbiculare*, a rich rose with the typical bell-shaped flowers. This flowers early in May. Finally there is Bowbells, flowering later in May with rose-pink flowers and lovely golden-brown young foliage. This comes out while the plant is still in flower, a charming combination.

There are also two dwarf pink hybrids that are worth growing. The first is Pink Drift (*scintillans* × *calostrotum*), with flowers like a slightly smaller edition of the latter parent carried in a three- to four-flowered truss. It is very free-flowering, and in its best forms is a good rose-pink, but it can also be tinged with magenta. The second is Fittra (*dauricum* × *racemosum*), It forms a low compact bush which is covered in late April with extremely vivid rose-pink flowers, of a shade that is unique among dwarfs. This is one of the few dwarfs that grows into a more shapely bush if it is completely dead-headed.

At the end we must include that pretty little plant called Spinulosum (*spinuliferum* × *racemosum*). In habit and foliage it is closer to the latter parent, but the flowers are apricot-pink with prominent stamens. It flowers in late April.

Yellows

The number of smaller-growing yellow hybrids is not large, nor are they completely hardy and suitable for any rock garden. Remo (*valentinianum* × *lutescens*) is compact in growth with bright-yellow flowers, but it is March-flowering. Valaspis (*valentinianum* × *leucaspis*) is bushy, usually about two feet high with creamy-yellow flowers, and is again March-flowering. We find Yellowhammer (*sulphureum* × *flavidum*) to be the hardiest, and a charming little plant, more upright in growth, with small foliage and little butter-yellow bells carried in threes and fours from terminal and axillary buds. It flowers in April.

Early flowering lepidote hybrids

There is a series of fairly dwarf hybrids that are possibly too early flowering for gardens in colder areas, but are very valuable for gardens that are frost-free in February and March. Most of them have got the February-flowering

R. moupinense and/or the March-flowering *R. ciliatum* for parents. The oldest and best known is certainly *R. x praecox* (*R. ciliatum* × *R. dauricum*), a compact bushy shrub up to five feet in height with very shiny green leaves and rosy-lilac flowers that appear in February. Even in a cold garden it is worth growing this charming plant. It comes into flower quickly during a mild spell.

A hybrid between it and *R. moupinense*, called Tessa, is smaller, only about three feet high with more pink in the colour of the flowers, with usually the addition of crimson spots. It is equally early, and possibly more suitable for the rock garden.

The tallest of this series is Bo-peep. From its parentage, *lutescens* × *moupinense*, this is only natural. It reaches 6 feet and is slender, not spreading. The flowers are comparatively large, appear in March and are creamy yellow with a deeper throat. Another March-flowering hybrid is Bric-a-Brac, *leucaspis* × *moupinense*, with 2-inch flowers, varying from pure white to pale pink. The white forms we consider to be superior. The last on our list is Cilpinense (*ciliatum* × *moupinense*), again March-flowering, which forms a round bush up to three feet high and across. The flowers are more bell-shaped and pinky white. This is probably the best except × *praecox* for colder gardens, as the bud sare frost-resistant, which is not always the case with the others in this early flowering group.

Hybrids of the Maddenii series

There is a group of hybrids, most of them made many years ago, of which the parents are members of the *Maddenii* and *Edgeworthii* series. While they can be grown in the west and south-west in sheltered positions, many of them also make first-class plants for house decoration when grown in large pots or tubs and trained round a framework of bamboo. If kept in a frost-free greenhouse they are very little trouble, and flower freely every year. The best for this purpose is undoubtedly Fragrantissimum (*edgeworthii* × *formosum*), which is about mid-way between both parents. Sesterianum is the same parentage. The flowers are white, tinted with pink, and are very fragrant. Equally good is the Countess of Haddington (*ciliatum* × *dalhousiae*), also white flushed rose towards the base. Lady Alice Fitzwilliam is very close but has often a faint lemon-yellow stain.

There are two, with *R. nuttallii* as a parent, with naturally more trumpet-shaped flowers. The better is Tyermanii, with *R. formosum* as the second parent, a fine plant and considerably hardier than *R. nuttallii*. The second is Victorianum, with *R. dalhousiae* as the second parent. In this case the hybrid is not so good as either of the parents but is a little hardier. Thus it has a certain value.

Diseases and Insect Pests

THE rhododendron as a whole is singularly free from major diseases and damage from insect pests. In the British Isles what trouble there is seems to be concentrated for the most part in the south of England, no doubt due to the higher summer temperatures. The farther north we go, the less is heard of pests and diseases until we arrive in our district on the east coast of Scotland, where the two major troubles, Bud Blast and the Rhododendron Fly, are so far unknown. Nor have there been any major attacks in the milder west coast of Scotland. This must surely indicate that a mild winter climate has nothing to do with them, but solely the summer temperature which will average ten or fifteen degrees higher in the south of England than in Scotland.

Of insect pests the Rhododendron Fly is the most important. The first stage in its life cycle is a dark-brown crawler without wings that always lives on the under-surface of the leaves. Later it turns into one of the Lacewing Flies. It lays its eggs after puncturing the under-surface of the leaves which become discoloured. The eggs hatch out at the start of summer.

If it were only a question of a few insects, the damage would not be worth talking about, but when they can be counted in their thousands, or rather cannot be counted because of their numbers, it can become a serious and damaging pest. The difficulty lies in spraying the under-surface of the leaves, as this has to be done thoroughly with a nicotine, derris or rotenone spray or powder. If you notice a series of yellow spots on the leaves followed by a sticky brown gum, it pays every time to make a careful examination and pick off and burn every leaf that shows damage. This may save an infestation the next year.

Other insect damage is negligible. There are reports of damage to early flowering varieties in the south from the Vine Weevil, and also the Clay-Coloured Weevil, the latter particularly on young plants in the nursery. We have also suffered minor damage during a dry June from caterpillars of various kinds, but this has always been on very young foliage. Whenever the leaves are more than half-open it seems to stop.

More serious secondary damage is caused by the Rhododendron Leaf Hopper, an insect like a minute grasshopper. This punctures the rhododendron bud which may let in the fungus spores that cause Bud Blast, a serious disease among some hybrids in the south. To look at Bud Blast is like frosted flower- and leaf-buds, but in spring the buds are covered with black hairs with tiny bulbs on their ends, smaller than pin heads. Other authorities blame frosted buds that are left on plants indefinitely. Whatever the cause an attack may be serious. At the moment there is no definite cure, but gardeners who have experienced attacks on their hybrids tell us that these can best be controlled by picking off every browned or discoloured bud during winter and burning them.

The only other fungus that may cause damage is the Honey Fungus, which attacks rhododendrons as it will attack any other hard wood. We have lost two plants in thirty-five years.

Lists of Species and Hybrids

KNOWING a little about rhododendrons and their behaviour, and having fairly decided views on what we like and do not like, we have spent some entertaining hours in making out lists of species and hybrids for various situations. We have then combined our lists and argued this way and that way until we have arrived at some kind of conclusion.

We would point out that these would all be our personal choice. Horticulture of all kinds would be incredibly dull if every gardener thought alike. We are therefore sure that many will object violently to many of our selections. We ourselves have often seen individual plants of species or hybrids that we have not included in our choice, but there has been some reason for this, usually because it has not been generally obtainable. What is the value of a list if the plant is so rare that it is only to be found in one garden and certainly not in the trade. Even then we feel that there must be many changes that others would like to see made. We repeat that these are our personal selections.

1 Twelve large species

auriculatum	white
barbatum	crimson-scarlet
calophytum	white or pale pink with crimson blotch
campanulatum	best forms lavender or white
decorum	white, fragrant
falconeri	creamy white or palest yellow
fictolacteum	white or pale rose with crimson blotch
hodgsonii	rose-purple
macabeanum	clear yellow with red blotch
sinogrande	creamy white with crimson blotch
sutchuenense	pale rose
thomsonii	blood-red

Lists of Species and Hybrids

2 Twelve species for warm and moist districts

arboreum	blood-red	*Jan - April*
bullatum	white, tinged pink, fragrant	*April - May*
burmanicum	greenish-yellow, fragrant	*April - May*
diaprepes	white	*July*
eriogynum	brightest red	*June*
griffithianum	white or cream, fragrant	*May*
lindleyi	white flushed rose, fragrant	*April*
macabeanum	clear yellow with red blotch	*March*
meddianum	deep crimson	*April*
rhabdotum	cream striped red	*May*
sinogrande	creamy white with crimson blotch	*April*
spinuliferum	brick-red	*April*

3 Twelve species for cooler and drier gardens

adenogynum	white flushed rose	*April*
campanulatum	lavender or white in good forms	*April*
decorum	white flushed pink, fragrant	*March - April - May*
desquamatum	pale or dark mauve	*April*
fargesii	pink	*April*
fictolacteum	white or pale rose, crimson blotch	*April*
fulvum	rose	*March - April*
griersonianum	geranium-scarlet	*June*
haematodes	scarlet-crimson	*May*
souliei	soft rose	*late May*
wardii	yellow	*May*
yunnanense	palest pink spotted red	*end of May*

4 Twelve hybrids for sheltered gardens

Cornish Cross	rose-pink
Fabia	orange-salmon
Grenadier	deep blood-red
Lady Bessborough	pale peach
Lady Chamberlain	salmon-pink to orange
Loderi	white or pale pink
Matador	scarlet
Naomi	pink-shaded green and lilac
Penjerrick	cream to pale pink or white
Polar Bear	white, fragrant
Shilsonii	blood-red
Tally-ho	scarlet

5 *Hybrids for colder gardens*

Betty Wormald	pale pink, pale purple blotch
Britannia	crimson
Christmas Cheer	pale pink
Fastuosum flore pleno	lavender-mauve
Goldsworth Yellow	apricot yellow
Loder's White	pink in bud fading white
Luscombei	pink
Mosers Maroon	maroon
Mrs Furnival	light pink, brown blotch
Mrs Lindsay Smith	white
Pink Pearl	pink
Purple Splendour	purple

6 *Twelve species and hybrids for smaller sheltered gardens*

aberconwayi	white tinged pink
Bowbells	pink
Earl of Athlone	blood-red
Elizabeth	blood-red
leucaspis	creamy white
moupinense	rose
neriiflorum	scarlet
spiciferum	bright pink
tephropeplum	deep rose
valentinianum	yellow
williamsianum	pink
Yellow Hammer	pale yellow

7 *Twelve species and hybrids for smaller cooler gardens*

Blue Diamond	blue
callimorphum	pink
carolinianum	rose or white
cuneatum	deep rose
Cunningham's Sulphur	pale yellow
dichroanthum	orange
Fittra	bright pink
glaucophyllum	pale rose
haematodes	scarlet-crimson
Praecox	rosy-lilac
racemosum	pink to white
sanguineum	deep red

Lists of Species and Hybrids

8   *Twelve early flowering species and hybrids*

Christmas Cheer	pale pink
ciliatum	white or palest rose
Cilpinense	white tinged pink
dauricum	rose-purple
fargesii	rose-pink
lutescens	yellow
moupinense	rose or white
mucronulatum	rose-purple
Nobleanum	scarlet-crimson
Praecox	rosy-lilac
strigillosum	scarlet-crimson
Tessa	pinkish-purple with red spots

9   *Twelve species with attractive, striking or unusual foliage*

bureavii	bright-brown indumentum
campanulatum var. *aeruginosum*	metallic sheen on young foliage
clementinae	steel-blue young foliage, white indumentum
falconeri	large leaves
lanatum	felted brown indumentum
lepidostylum	very glaucous young foliage
makinoi	narrow leaves, wooly tawny indumentum
mallotum	dense cinnamon-brown indumentum
orbiculare	round foliage, glaucous
roxieanum	very narrow felted leaves
sinogrande	the largest rhododendron leaves
williamsianum	bronze young foliage, almost round

10   *Twelve medium-sized species*

augustinii	blue	*early May*
caeruleum var. *album*	white	*May*
campylocarpum	yellow	*April - May*
cerasinum	cherry-red or white or a mixture	*end April*
chaetomallum	deep crimson	*March - April*
cinnabarinum	yellow, orange or cinnabar red	*May - June*
griersonianum	geranium-scarlet	*June*
insigne	palest pink	*May to June*
neriiflorum	scarlet	*April*
orbiculare	rose	*April*
pseudoyanthinum	bright red-purple	*April - May*
souliei	soft rose	*late May*

187

11 *Twelve larger dwarfs usually over two feet high*

calostrotum	magenta *May - June*
campylogynum	pink to plum-purple *May*
chamae-thomsonii	soft pink or red
fastigiatum	bright purple
hippophaeoides	best forms lavender *April*
racemosum	shades of pink *March - April - May*
russatum	deep purple-blue *April - May*
scintillans	deep lavender-blue *early April*
tephropeplum	deep rose *April may*
trichostomum	white or rose
valentinianum	yellow *April*
williamsianum	pink *April.*

12 *Twelve dwarf or prostrate species usually under two feet high*

camtschaticum	reddish-purple *May*
cephalanthum	
var. *crebreflorum*	pink *May*
chryseum	yellow *April - May*
forrestii	scarlet-crimson *April - May*
hanceanum	pale yellow *April*
idoneum	deep blue-purple with white throat
impeditum	deep blue-purple *April - May*
intricatum	lavender *April - May*
microleucum	white *April*
pemakoense	pinkish-purple *April*
radicans	purple *May*
sargentianum	yellow or cream *May*

Index

Series, Subseries and Varieties of Rhododendrons

All references to pages 149–64 are Azaleas
Page numbers in italics indicate illustrations

Index

Printed in Great Britain by
Thomas Nelson and Sons Ltd, Edinburgh